In the Beginning
It Was Not So

[Handwritten inscription at top] 7/2021 Dr. Peggy & Carmine. God allowed us to meet. We are all Blessed Stay Blessed *[signature]*

In the Beginning It Was Not So

Seven Marriage Lessons Learned in the Garden

[Handwritten inscription] To Carmine And Peggy, It was a pleasure meeting you Both. We have new friends! May God Bless you Both as you continue To follow God's design for Life, Love, and marriage! The Garden Model! Terry 7/2021

TERRY AND CAROL MOSS

XULON PRESS ELITE

Xulon Press Elite
2301 Lucien Way #415
Maitland, FL 32751
407.339.4217
www.xulonpress.com

Paperback ISBN-13: 978-1-6628-2107-3
Hard Cover ISBN-13: 978-1-6628-2348-0
Ebook ISBN-13: 978-1-6628-2108-0

Table of Contents

Acknowledgments

To God, our Father: our heartfelt thanks for the inspiration to complete this work. It was a long-time coming but the result very appreciated. We are in awe of your amazing grace and love continuously granted to us. May our lives lived daily reflect our love back to you.

(Terry) So much to thank my darling wife for. Thank you for your encouragement, support, and understanding shown to me during the countless hours of focused isolation typing away in our study. Thank you also for being a living example of what a "suitable helper" looks like and feels like. You are a tremendous blessing to my life, our home, and our love every day. I am often humbled when thinking of how wonderfully blessed I am. I am so glad God gave me one of his best daughters as that "helper" suitable for me!

To Christopher and Jacque Falconer: your friendship of over 25 years has been a constant blessing to my life. Through all that life has thrown our respective ways, our friendship, love, and respect for each other has never waned. Thank you both for your constant support and encouragement of both me and Carol, for the work we do in our ministry to couples countrywide. May God continue to bless you richly. I am honored to call you our true friends. Love you both!

(Carol) To my loving Husband: thank you for being an amazing husband. I am so proud of your accomplishments and for your obedience in writing this book. For years I have heard of your dreams and now seeing your success makes my heart smile. Thank you for inviting me to share this dream with you. I am a truly blessed wife because God has given me a genuine man of God who carries the true spirit of God and who understands how to love me as commanded in 1 Corinthians 13:4-8. You have used your past experiences to become better and not bitter.

Your love for both me and our children has been a beacon of light in times of despair. You work hard every day to make me smile and fulfill my dreams. You have pushed me out of my comfort zone to become a spiritual leader even more than I could have ever imagined. Because of your love and Godly leadership, you have helped me grow closer to God and my purpose. I thank God for giving me the loving, caring, and understanding husband I have always wanted and prayed for.

To all the couples everywhere who have been individually counseled by us, taught by us, mentored, coached, cajoled by us; those of you who have experienced "the blue chairs" because, well, you needed it! To all of you who have trusted us, encouraged us, recommended us, vouched for us, supported, and loved us-Thank you! You all have a part in the making of this book. You all have given us the opportunity to sharpen our focus, to clarify our purpose, and prepare us for the opportunities God has given us. We love you all!

To all our children and grandchildren: what a blessing and a privilege we have been given to be Dad, Mom, "Stepdad", "Stepmom", Grand Pa, and Grandma Carol. Each precious role has given us the opportunity to learn and grow. We are better for it. We love you all immensely!

To Doreen Ernandez: we cannot thank you enough for the countless hours you spent pouring over every word, sentence, and detail of our manuscript while editing it for excellence. Your compassionate heart and love for us and our work, was such a blessing and encouragement. Your keen eye for details and your meticulous quest for getting every detail right, was reassuring throughout the editing process. You have truly earned your "Eagle-Eye" nickname! We are eternally grateful for the opportunity to have worked with you!

Finally, thank you Gina and the Xulon Press Team. Gina was used by God to inspire us, direct us, and encourage us to go forward even when there was doubt in ourselves and our ability to write this book. What a comfort it was to know we had the "Team" behind us and helping us along the way. May God bless you all!

Foreword

There are people and events in your life you will never forget because of their impact. Such was the case when I first met and was smitten by my wife Jacqueline at the National Commercial Bank Atrium building in Kingston, Jamaica in December 1989.

Also was the case when meeting a young Sunday School teacher named Terry Moss in calendar year 1996, an event ranked highly in my life because it has been impactful to my spiritual life and marriage of 25 years.

I first met Terry Moss, when at the urging and invitation of my wife Jacqueline, then a new "born again" Christian, I attended a Sunday School class titled "Man in the Mirror" that was taught by Terry at a kindergarten school that served as a temporary place of worship for my wife's Church that was under construction. As a man 6 foot two inches tall, I remembered sitting in a kindergarten classroom on a small uncomfortable classroom chair asking myself "why did you let your wife talk you into this."

However, those thoughts did not last for long because minutes into the Sunday School class I observed a passionate teacher who was relatable and who skillfully shared the Bible and made it practical to my life. It goes without saying, I did not miss a class and months later I confessed Jesus as my Lord and Savior and was baptized, starting a personal relationship with Jesus. Terry Moss quickly became a friend and confidant to my wife Jacqueline and me. Later, I was privileged to serve with him and observe his dynamic leadership on our Church's Trustee Board and his oratory skills as an assistant Pastor at our local Church in New Jersey.

Jacqueline and I have been privileged to know Terry and his wife Carol as friends and Spiritual Advisors and are humbled to be asked to write the Foreword for their book *"In the Beginning It Was Not So-Seven Marriage Lessons Learned in the Garden."*

This book offers cogent evidence to support the authors' arguments and propositions. It is so typical of the insightful and inspirational work/ministries of Terry and Carol, including "One Flesh Ministries" and "Marriage Enrichment Moments."

Most importantly, the book took us on a journey toward marital enlightenment and fulfillment from a biblical perspective.

Our hope and prayer is that this book will have the same impact on your life as it has impacted ours.

Christopher and Jacqueline Falconer

Introduction by the Authors

There are many books written about marriage and divorce. So why would we write yet another book on these subjects? That's a good question. As a matter of fact, we asked ourselves the same question.

For many years it has been suggested that we write a book. That suggestion has come from pastors, ministry leaders, family members, co-workers, and professional service providers–after engaging in brief relationship focused discussions, and a myriad of couples we have been blessed to counsel, coach, and mentor over the years.

But why us? Why this book? Why now? All great questions.

Why us? The best answer we can give to that question is because we have a compassionate heart to help couples build healthy marriage relationships. Additionally, together we have been ministering to couples for nearly 15 years and Terry has been ministering to couples for over 25 years.

(Terry) These 25 years of counseling, coaching, mentoring, teaching, and training couples have seared into my mind many of the issues that are making marriage harder than the designer (Our Father and Creator of the Universe) first intended.

During these years there have been many hurting couples counseled, who are not experiencing the deep-down-in-your-soul joy that a healthy, fulfilling marriage relationship brings. These hurting couples are like bleating lambs crying out for help that seemingly never comes. I want our heavenly Father to use the heart and experience He has instilled in us, to help stop the crying that comes from these hurting lambs.

In addition, there is my own personal journey including a previous marriage of 26 years that ended in divorce. Then there was a brief but significant period of "finding myself" and gaining a much clearer understanding of what makes real relationships work. I want to share those learned insights with as many couples as possible.

(Carol) After experiencing domestic violence which led to a divorce, there was a "preparation" period for me as well. It was a time in which I learned a lot about myself and about what really makes relationships work. Being a strong independent woman (by nature), I had to learn how to "submit" to my husband with love and respect. This term is often misconstrued and misrepresented. But as God worked in me to be the industrious, respectful, genuine, servant-hearted leader he intended for me to be, I found "submitting" to my husband to be "second-nature." (Read *What Submission Really Means* in Chapter 10 of this book).

God prepared his best in me, to be the best of me, so that I could be the best person to the man whom He sent me to be his "suitable" helper. Because the man God gave to me loves and cherishes me, I am free to love him, come alongside him, and yes, even submit myself to his leadership. It is a wonderful gift to give to the man I love. My hope is that you will allow the learned lessons in this book to show you how to share that gift with your husband as well.

(Both) God conferred upon us a great gift of love and grace when He gave us a "second chance" to love again. He brought us together (with our unique differences) and taught us how to unselfishly, and unconditionally, do marriage differently than either of us had experienced before. We now want to share what we have learned along the way.

In addition to bringing our own experiences and learnings to this work, we have learned a lot from other people's experiences as well. Over the nearly fifteen years that we have been married we have had the tremendous opportunity to engage with hundreds of couples who have expressed (and demonstrated) tremendous angst in trying to figure out how to do marriage right.

It became apparent to us that we needed to share some of the insights we have gained through the years, to benefit many couples who really want a healthy, thriving, and fulfilling marriage relationship, yet have not been able to experience it. Sadly, many of us have not seen enough models of such relationships to know how to emulate them. We hope this book will help by providing the guidance you need to **be** the models of that kind of relationship.

Our children are watching us. We must BE the models!

Why this book? This book has been in the making for over 25 years. Year after year of counseling couples having deep heart-wrenching relationship issues, has taught us a thing or two. Over those years of counseling coaching, and mentoring couples, and individuals, from all walks of life, from various cultures and ethnicities, from across America and beyond; most couples have told us they don't know how to do relationship well because they simply have not seen many, if any, good relationship models to go by.

As we became more skillful "students of people", and "students of the Word", we realized there was a clear model of success for marriage, detailed in the beginning, in the Garden.

As couples started experiencing these transformative changes from this "Garden Model", we began hearing things like, "you two have saved our marriage"; "you two need a broader platform" to share this with more people; and "more people need to get the kind of help you two provide."

This book is an inspired work that gives a glimpse into the Designer's (God) intent for marriage. In each learned lesson our quest is to show you revealed truth that provides you another necessary ingredient for enjoying the beauty of a fulfilling marriage relationship, as it was in the beginning.

In each learned lesson, be a seeker of revelation and not just information. This book is not a biblical study of scripture to gain a deeper knowledge of the Word. That may happen, but also use this as an opportunity to broaden your understanding of the model we can follow to have more flourishing marriage relationships.

Information *informs* us, revelation *transforms* us. May this book transform you as you uncover truth about how the Designer initially intended marriage relationships to be.

One caution, even with this revealed truth, each couple and each person still must do the work necessary to bring transformative change within themselves.

Why now? It's time! We have seen enough and learned enough to clearly understand and, hopefully, clearly articulate the principles that produce the necessary mind-shift and heart-shift, that creates healthy, loving, and joy filled marriage relationships.

After all, that is God's design and desire for us all… "that your joy will be full!" (John 15:11)

The quality of relationships (marriage or otherwise) is at an all-time low. There is so much discord, disconnect, and discontent in the hearts and minds of people everywhere. This is a universal problem affecting the entirety of our world. It is not a problem isolated to one group of people, or one race, or one nation. It is a human race problem affecting us all.

But the solution to this universal problem requires something of us that we cannot provide using the framework of our own conscience. There must be something more, something deeper, and something universally transforming. We believe the model for such transformation comes by having an insight into what the Creator envisioned relationships to be in the beginning.

The universal relationship problems we are experiencing today - "In the beginning it was not so!"

In this book *"In the Beginning It Was Not So"* we will take a venture back to the "beginning" (Genesis-the Book of "Beginnings") to get a clearer look at how God intended marriage to work. We will extract from Adam and Eve's experiences in the Garden of Eden seven key "learnings" that can transform our thinking and our relationships in real impactful ways.

We will start with understanding our own purpose in life. We will discuss how this impacts our view of ourselves and our self-worth. This is an important first step in a person's ability to completely give themself to another in relationship. Absent of this self-awareness and self-acceptance, a person could look to a spouse to fulfill that part of them. This was not intended in the beginning and leads to problems in current day relationships.

Three "learnings" we will discuss surrounds one very significant "creature", and that is the WOMAN! The woman's companionship is man's greatest need, and she is also his greatest challenge. This woman is not like ANY of the other creatures God made and that Adam had the responsibility to name. Yet, it is that "uniqueness" of who she is that poses so many moments of confusion and frustration for men today who really are trying to love and understand her.

Today (unlike in the beginning), the man's sheer ignorance of her, causes the woman to withdraw into her own emotional shell of confusion and isolation, and thus the difficulties begin. But in the beginning, it was not so. We will attempt to provide guidance from the Garden, that affords couples a way out of this circle of uncertainty, to a place of peace and fulfillment.

Finally, we will look at the "path to oneness" that was so carefully and specifically laid out for us by the Creator himself. We all want and need oneness in our relationship to feel the fulfillment God designed. Yet today, there is a "disrupter" lurking in and around all marriage relationships just waiting to divide us, so that he may conquer. Embracing the learned lessons in this book, will help thwart the sinister plot against every marriage relationship.

Therefore, let us begin our journey together toward marital enlightenment, instruction, and inspiration. Let us go back to "the beginning" where there was blissful innocence, pure committed relationships, and oneness of heart, mind, and purpose.

We will go back to the Garden of Eden, from where our seven marriage lessons originate.

Before we do that, we must explore the question, that triggered the response, that imparted the wisdom, that has the potential to change the course of your marriage and that of future generations.

We must first deal with... the *divorce issue*.

Authors' Note:

Although Carol co-authored this book, the primary "voice" is that of Terry. Carol has added important insight, suggestions, and "color" to the finished work. Her impact is also woven in the fabric of this work throughout each page and chapter. When Carol's "voice" is primary that change will be shown through parentheses with her name identified.

What They Are Saying

As we read *In the Beginning It Was Not So*, we felt like we were sitting around the table laughing with Terry and Carol as we did in our premarital mentoring before beginning our blended family journey. So many of the concepts and tools they shared with us in those life-shaping sessions are given full scope in this book. It is a beautiful, natural overflowing of not only their many years of experience, but also who they are as people: personable, insightful, fun, and willing to tell it like it is! If you're married or want to be, read this book! It will change the way you see yourself, respond to your spouse, and cherish your marriage.

Aaron and Rachel Wheeler
Student Ministries Director
River Valley Christian Fellowship
Bourbonnais, Illinois

Terry and Carol are WONDERFUL. Two very loving and gifted people that are willing to show their imperfections and help others wade through the ups and downs of life. They have a lot of wisdom, life experience and just fun personalities. You both have been blessed to lead and teach others in a fun and kind way, being authoritative when necessary but always loving and kind. You two are gems and I have enjoyed our time together! Thank you so much.

Andrea Dobbins
Marriage Enrichment Class Attendee
Palm Beach Gardens, Florida

My Husband and I started off our relationship with Terry and Carol Moss, and they are a true godsend. Every group, personal interaction, and personal conversation has been heartfelt and with love, even at times it being "tough love." They are the most loving, caring, encouraging, thoughtful, selfless couple that we have ever met.

Arion and Tina Dawson
Marriage Intensive Recipient
Crest Hill, Illinois

CHAPTER 1

The Divorce Issue
(Matthew 19:3-8)

D ivorce and remarriage are pervasive issues today. The tragedy of shattered homes and crushed hearts is seen more and more often in our society, even within the church.

According to an online article in the World Population Review:

(https://worldpopulationreview.com/), Marriage and divorce are both common experiences for adults, although both can be challenging. About 90% of people in Western cultures marry by age 50. In the United States, about 50% of married couples divorce, the sixth-highest divorce rate in the world. Subsequent marriages have an even higher divorce rate: 60% of second marriages end in divorce and 73% of all third marriages end in divorce.

Divorces can be emotionally and financially difficult. They can greatly affect parents as well as the couple's children.

As much as we all want a happy ending to marriage, divorce is sometimes thought to be the only path for some couples.

The divorce rate in the US is going down, but not because couples are deciding to stay together. On the contrary, they are just not getting married at all. With a slew of issues connected to divorce, such as staggering costs and ugly child custody battles, couples are delaying marriage out of divorce fears.

The following statistics were created by CompareCamp.com in a May 6, 2020 online article (https://comparecamp.com/divorce-statistics/divorce-statistics-main/).

They cite various statistics that impact the decision to divorce:

*58% of Americans believe that divorce is much better than staying together in an unhappy marriage.

*73% see divorce as morally acceptable.

*Infidelity is the top reason for divorce.

*1 in 3 divorces starts as an online affair.

*Pornography – one study observed that men who started watching porn increased their risk of divorce from 5% to 10%; for women, it was from 6% to 18%.

*56% of divorce cases involve one party having an obsessive interest in pornographic websites.

*Millennial divorce is a declining divorce rate; however, this may not be a cause for celebration. That is because a deeper dive into the statistics reveals that there are fewer marriages to begin with, as millennials wait longer to get married or not marry at all.

*"Gray Divorces" are on the rise among older people between 50 and 65. The usual assumption that major life transitions like an "empty nest" or retirement fuel gray divorces have no strong correlation. Instead, the same reasons found in most divorces

in younger people—quality of marriage—is also salient for older couples.

*The divorce rate for people aged 50 and above has doubled since the 1990s. For people aged 65 and above, the rate has tripled.

*55% of gray divorces involve couples who have been married for 20 years.

*Remarried couples are also 2.5 times more likely to divorce compared to couples in a first marriage; thus, ending in a gray divorce.

*People who went through a gray divorce had worse feelings of depression versus those whose spouses died.

Statistics are simply numbers. Yet, behind each number is a person or persons that must deal with the emotional turmoil that may come with divorce.

So, what is the answer? What can be done to reduce the number of divorces and the emotional impact on couples, children, and society as a whole? Is avoiding marriage altogether the key to relationship happiness?

Perhaps looking at the issue differently might be a good place to start.

The Encyclopedia of Bible Words provides in the definition of marriage, the "covenant character of marriage." It states, the Old Testament (OT) introduces marriage as a lifelong link between two persons. The two so share their lives that they become one in their experience here on earth.

Many OT allusions make it clear that in marriage the commitment of husband and wife to each other reflects God's covenant commitment to His people. God has made two one: each partner is to preserve the commitment that makes marriage the enriching relationship that God intends (Malachi 2:15).

This definition of marriage, which describes marriage as a "covenant", just may begin to shed light on the solve for this issue of divorce.

The question is, **is divorce REALLY the issue?**

Do not get me wrong, yes, as outlined above, divorce is certainly *an* issue. The question to ponder however, is whether divorce is really *the* issue.

Keep reading as we seek to uncover a way to reduce divorces and, more importantly, improve covenantal marriage relationships from the very beginning.

A Side Note:

This book begins by addressing the divorce issue that has ended an estimated 50% of the marriages in the United States and even more in other countries. Marriage is a relationship that is meant to be enjoyed not endured. Yet, in an April 28, 2020 online article in Marriage.com blogger Sylvia Smith states, "If you're not exactly blissful and happy in your marriage, you are not alone. Only 60 percent of people are happy in their unions." (https://www.marriage.com/advice/relationship/reasons-for-an-unhappy-marriage/).

However, although we start with the need to address the divorce issue (as you will understand why as you read on), the issues that lead to divorce are the same reasons many marriages are unhealthy and unfulfilling even though the couples remain together.

The learnings detailed in this book will ultimately benefit both groups. This book will help couples avoid divorce, and more importantly, for couples getting married, or those who remain married, will show them what is required to enjoy a healthy, mutually satisfying, God-honoring marriage, both so desperately want and deserve to have. After all, isn't that why we get married in the first place?

1A. The Big Question – Is it "Lawful?" *(verses 3-6)*

There is no question that God's ideal for marriage is that of an unbroken covenant: a lifelong relationship that mirrors on earth God's faithfulness to those whom he has chosen to love.

In Jesus' time there was a debate over the exact conditions under which a divorce might be lawfully granted. Was divorce allowed only in the event of adultery, or could a divorce be obtained also for incompatibility? (e.g., for "any and every reason") [Matthew 19:3].

Among the people of Jesus' day, there were both conservative and liberal views of divorce taught by the rabbis. The liberal perspective said a man could divorce his wife for almost any reason - including if she burned his dinner. The Pharisees wanted Jesus to take a side to stir up controversy.

Pharisees [FAIR-uh-sees] were a small but extremely influential lay fellowship of men committed (1) to strictly observe all the ordinances of Judaism, and (2) to scrupulously carry out religious duties. The Gospels portray the Pharisees as antagonists of Jesus.

Although the conditions were debated, there was no doubt that OT law permitted divorce.

Jesus did not offer a mere opinion, though. He pointed them to God's Word. He showed them that the only reason they were posing a question about divorce, is because **they did not understand marriage.**

A lack of understanding will produce ignorance due to our overall blindness to the deeper truth.

Before we can talk about divorce, then, we need to understand what marriage is. What does the Scripture say? In the beginning God made them male and female (Genesis 1:27). At the dawn of creation, God made one man for one woman, with no escape hatch.

When the Pharisees tried to involve Jesus in this debate over the legalities, Jesus reaffirmed the sanctity of the marriage covenant. Still his questioners probed. "Why then did Moses command that a man give his wife a certificate of divorce and send her away?" (Matthew 19:7, New International Version).

Jesus' response is profound and provides key principles for later discussion in this book.

"Moses permitted you to divorce your wives because your hearts were hard" (Matthew 19:8).

Jesus' point is that sin (sinful pride and selfishness) warps the most sacred of relationships. Humanity, in the grip of sin's hardening power, can twist the wonderful gift of marriage. Its healing and enriching design can be distorted into a warped parody that crushes and destroys.

Hence, sin, that started from the beginning, still preys upon the heart of man to deny the sacredness of God's greatest blessing to man, a covenant marriage relationship.

Divorce is by no means the best solution to marital problems today, nor was it so in biblical times. Divorce is not God's will for a couple, even if adultery is involved!

God's solution is forgiveness and continuing love, which mirrors the Lord's own faithfulness to us despite untold hurts.

But there will sometimes be relationships in which one partner or the other *will not* respond to love and will reject commitment to the other. In such cases, in which heart commitment to covenant love is consistently rejected, a legal divorce may follow.

In such cases it is not the divorce that is the sin, but the sin that necessitates the divorce; the sin of selfishness and pride (more on this later). Which then leads to hostility, unfairness, dishonesty, disloyalty, oppression, cruelty, and apathy regarding the marriage relationship.

God, then, has provided divorce for those whose marriages have already been destroyed by the hardness of a human heart.

We should note here that hardness of heart has many aspects. It need not suggest active hostility. Like other sins, hardness of heart may simply involve a falling short, a callousness of ignorance, per se. This callousness, however, ***creates an inability for the heart to give and receive love.***

The inability to give and receive love is probably the greatest destroyer of marriages today. Many couples have shared with us that they simply do not know how to do love and marriage God's way. Many of these couples (about 98% in our very own "unscientific" research poll), admit they do not know how, because they had very few to no models of successful marriages to go by in their family of origin, religious circles, or among close friends who were married.

Therefore, we have a generation of couples who live in frustrated marriages because they do not have the covenantal love they want (or expect), because they do not know how to give it to another.

You cannot give what you do not have. And you cannot get, what you do not give.

This internal frustration then causes you to fight (quarrel, complain, criticize, etc.) to get the love you want but do not get, which creates anxiety, stress, bitterness, and anger. This then causes "hardness of the heart" because you cannot get what you want, because you do not yet know how to get beyond yourself to show Godly love to the other. We then throw up our hands, consider the situation to be hopeless, and determine the problem is "unreconcilable differences." What a major challenge this is in so many marriage relationships today!

When Jesus was questioned about divorce, he pointed back to the ideal established at the time of creation: "Haven't you read that at the beginning the Creator 'made them male and female' and said, "For this reason a man will leave his father and mother and be united to his wife, and the two will become one flesh"? (more detail on this provided in learned Lesson #7). "So they are no longer two, but one flesh. Therefore, what God has joined together, let no one separate." (Matthew 19:4-6, NIV).

In Matthew 19, Jesus further points out that the Pharisees' concern with legalities misses the true and deeper issue: *failure to achieve God's ideal.* Matthew 18 presents principles for healing

8

hurts in intimate relationships. But the Pharisees were not concerned with hurts or with ideals. They cared only about legal technicalities.

How often, even today, is there more of a concern with the "look" of divorce, and the perception others may have, rather than real concern and care for the ones experiencing the hurt and pain of the divorce.

It is here that Jesus points out that divorce was permitted because human hearts are hard, not because God desires divorce.

Divorce was an expression of God's mercy, not an affirmation of his ideal will.

In the New Testament, in both I Corinthians 7 and Romans 7:2-3, Paul deals with the issue of divorce by again addressing the critical question… is it (probably more emphatically stated is it not?), the leaving – the abandonment of the marriage – the controlling circumstance? As Paul discussed specific relational circumstances (7:13), it seems that the controlling circumstance is *abandonment of the covenant relationship* by one of the partners in the marriage.

In Romans 7:2-3, it seems that a refusal to live as a married person, like death of one partner, breaks the covenant bond and releases the willing partner to remarry.

But again, to be clear, divorce is not God's best desire for His people. Those who are able and willing to live in God's way within the marriage relationship will not divorce. There will be no need or desire to do so.

Stated another way, the problem, or the real issue, is not divorce, the problem is the choices people make to abandon the covenant relationship because they are not willing to do it God's way or have never learned how to do so. But ***in the beginning, it was not so.***

We believe the information detailed in the balance of this book will provide helpful guidance as to the "how to" do marriage relationships God's way, the way He, the Designer, originally intended. But you will still have to provide the "want to."

Let it be said here, and it may be said again, the guidance provided in this book, and the encouragement to remain in your covenant relationship (your marriage), is not intended for those in abusive relationships. In those circumstances, get help or get out!

1B. The REAL Problem – Pride and Selfishness *(verses 7-8a)*

"Why then did Moses command a man give his wife a certificate of divorce and send her away?" (Matthew 19:7).

As stated earlier, Jesus' response is important, and provides key principles for consideration. "Moses permitted you to divorce your wives because *your hearts were hard*, but in the beginning, it was not so" (Matthew 19:8).

This significant point must be understood in the context of the "covenant character of marriage." A person's heart becomes "hard", or experiences "hardness" in a marriage relationship when due to sinful pride, stubbornness, or selfishness, one or the other is no longer committed to the covenant agreement as confirmed by these behaviors.

The love, respect, and commitment to the other is no longer the person's interest, priority, or desire. When this occurs, the "covenant character" of the relationship has been broken because their interest has selfishly become all about them and their needs and wants.

As we unpack this issue of pride a bit, let it be said that there is a difference between "sinful pride" and "good pride." To keep things simple, let us define "good pride" as a person being proud of their accomplishments, with humility and honest recognition of the favor and grace provided.

On the flip side, we can look at "sinful pride", or the type of pride that brings challenge to any relationship, as follows:

Characteristics/Behaviors of "Sinful Pride":

Critical, Negative, Always right, Dictatorial, Greed, Fearful, Worry, Impatient, Interruptive, Self-righteous, Obstinate, Egotistical, Contentious, Boastful, Smug, Selfish, Strife, Boasting, Competition, and Wrong motives.

When you understand these characteristics of "sinful pride", it is easy to see how this insufferable internal characteristic can easily produce a negative consequence in any relationship. This sinful pride makes it difficult for the person with this characteristic to fully give themselves to another person, because many of these characteristics are from the selfish or self-focused perspective.

A "covenant marriage", centered in God's love, is by definition "others-centered", not "self-centered". It is self-sacrificing (like Christ's love for us) and motivated from a desire to please the other person over yourself.

Note that, while we only have one word for love, the ancient Greeks in their pursuit of wisdom and self-understanding, found eight different varieties of love that we all experience at some point. The most common of these are "Eros", or erotic love; "Philia", or affectionate love; "Storge", or familiar love; and "Agape", or selfless love.

The highest and most radical type of love according to the Greeks is agape, or selfless unconditional love.

This type of love is not the sentimental outpouring that often passes as love in our society. It has nothing to do with the condition-based type of love that our sex-obsessed culture tries to pass as love.

Agape is what some call spiritual love. It is an unconditional love, bigger than yourself, boundless compassion, an infinite empathy. It is the purest form of love that is free from desires and expectations; and loves regardless of the flaws and shortcomings of others.

Agape is the love that is felt for that which we intuitively know as the divine truth: the love that accepts, forgives, and believes for our greater good.

What does it really mean to love someone? Ancient Greek gives us some insight. Jesus said, "Do to others what you would want them to do to you" (Luke 6:31). This is a restatement of something else Jesus said in the Gospel of Mark, "Love your neighbor as yourself". (Mark 12:31)

The point here is, loving one another in marriage relationships, as defined by the ancient Greeks, is not selfish, prideful, or sinful. What it is, however, is others-centered, self-sacrificing, and motivated by a desire to please the other person over yourself.

Do you think if we really loved our spouses this way, they would ever feel like differences were "irreconcilable", or would feel the need to bring up the "D" word? What if this kind of love is demonstrated in all our relationships; what a world this would be! (Well, we can hope, can't we?). (See *How Love Behaves* in Chapter 10 of this book).

It is good to often remind oneself that "God resists the proud but gives grace to the humble." (James 4:6).

Humility is the antidote to pride. (See *10 Ways to Reflect God's Humility* in Chapter 10 of this book).

Let us continue the discussion around pride and selfishness:

Selfishness: According to Psychology Today, there are three distinct types of selfish actions: the good, the bad, and the neutral. John Johnson, PhD, a former professor of psychology at Pennsylvania State University, says that whenever you are not sure if your actions veer too far toward greediness, the question to ask yourself is this: "Who's benefiting from my 'selfish' behavior?"

You can scrutinize your motivation a bit more with the three buckets of selfishness:

"Good selfishness": Dr. Johnson says that this type is a mutually beneficial, win-win situation for both parties involved.

"Let us say, for example, that you and your friend's favorite purveyor of athleisure is having a buy one, get one deal on leggings. Just split the cost of the first pair right down the middle—and bam—you both walk away with fresh yoga attire. It's selfish, but hey—it's selfish rocking a new pair of tights".

"Neutral selfishness": "Neutral selfishness includes looking after your own well-being in ways that do not directly and substantially involve other people," says the psychologist. If you are a living, breathing, yearning human being, you have been neutrally selfish at least a couple times today. Simply brushing your teeth, making yourself dinner, or participating in any self-care activity falls under this category.

"Bad selfishness": If you have ever done something that only benefits one person on the planet (i.e., yourself) then you have been bad selfish. "Ultimately this behavior is bad for both the selfish person and the people victimized and exploited by the selfish person," Dr. Johnson explains.

In an online article by Corina Dondas in ALLWOMENSTALK.com (SEP 06, 2019), she described selfish people as having the following traits:

"The traits of a selfish individual aren't easy to notice since they often seem really nice, lovable and sweet people. Really though, a selfish person only tries to satisfy their own pleasures, they have little consideration for other people's needs and they worry only about their own comfort.

Most selfish people are skilled manipulators by instinct who believe that they are more important than everyone else. They can hurt you very easily and you might feel confused and lost when you're around them because they make you feel like you aren't giving enough back to them."

Dondas goes on to state, "Here are a few obvious signs of a selfish person that you should pay attention to:

1. THEY ALWAYS ASK FOR FAVORS

One of the most obvious signs of a selfish person is the fact that they always ask for favors, no matter how big or small they are. They always need something from you, but they are never willing to give you something back in return. Try asking them for a favor and see if they are willing to help you.

2. THEY THINK THEY DESERVE SPECIAL TREATMENT

A selfish individual will always think that they deserve special treatment and that is why they will ask you for all kinds of favors even if you do not know them so well. They often think that they are better than everyone else and they are not afraid of saying that out loud.

3. THEY ARE VERY FRIENDLY

Selfish people are often very friendly, nice, and caring people, especially when they first meet someone. You could even say that they are people pleasers, but once you will get to know them, you will notice their lazy and aloof side. They often pamper and care for you until you drop your guard down and you welcome them into your life.

4. THEY USE OTHERS

Selfish people use others all the time and they are not afraid of admitting it. They might even share a laugh with you and tell you how they used one of their friends or even their partner to make them do something for them. They do not even realize that what they are doing is wrong because they consider themselves to be special and they think that others should do everything they can to make them happy.

5. **THEY BARELY SAY THANK YOU**

When you do a selfish friend a favor, they will barely say thank you and even then, they will sound insincere. They are not that grateful for what you have done for them since they think that they deserve special treatment from everyone else. Try asking them for a favor and you will see that they brush it off and that they will never follow through with it.

6. **YOU CAN SPOT THEIR FAKENESS**

You can spot a selfish individual's fakeness, especially when they talk to others. They will go over the top to be nice and friendly with them, even though you know that they really dislike them and that they do not care about those people's needs. They often appear to be sweet, but you know that their behavior is insincere and that they are only trying to use you.

7. **THEY TRY TO CONFUSE YOU**

A selfish friend will often try to confuse you, to make you doubt your value as a true friend. Selfish people are skilled manipulators who can make you think that you are not doing enough for them or that you are not cool enough and that you need to try harder.

In understanding the traits of a selfish person, it is obvious how difficult it would be to remain in a meaningful relationship with anyone like this.

A selfish person ends up losing friends or loved ones because no matter how charming or interesting a selfish person may be, a relationship with a selfish person is hard to maintain. *A truly selfish person would never consider the possibility that they are selfish.* If you are worried that you are too prideful or selfish, and want to be on the path to gratitude and humility, then there are several things you can do: (Co-authored by Klare Heston, LCSW)

1. **Practice putting yourself last.** If you are a selfish person, then chances are that you are always looking for #1, well, first. You have got to change that as soon as you can if you want to start living a life filled with joy and free of selfishness. The next time you are doing something, whether you are in line at a buffet or waiting for your seat on the bus, stop and let other people have what they want first, whether it is food, comfort, or ease. Do not be the person who always thinks *me, me, me* and must get everything first. Remember that other people are every bit as special as you are, and that other people deserve to get what they want too.

2. **Put yourself in someone else's shoes.** Walking a mile in another man's shoes can change your life for eternity. Of course, you will not be able to do this, but you can put in the effort into thinking about the other people around you and considering how they might be feeling in any given situation. Consider how your mother, your friend, your boss, or a random person on the street may be feeling before you act, and you may find that the world is not as clean cut as you thought it was. The more you practice empathy and wondering what other people are going through, the sooner you will be able to give up your selfishness.

3. **Remember that you are not more important than anyone else.** Selfish people are constantly thinking that they are the center of the universe and that the world should revolve around them. Well, you need to drop that thought like a bad habit. Whether you are Madonna or Donna the hairdresser, you should think of yourself as the same as everyone else, not as somehow better because you have more money, more looks, or more talent than the person standing next to you.

4. **Don't let your past dictate your future.** Okay, so maybe all your friends, coworkers, and neighbors think of you as the most selfish person in the world. You may be finding it difficult to break out of that pattern or to have other people view you as something other than what they expected you to be. Well, stop thinking that way and learn to move forward and to become a new person. Sure, other people who know you may be surprised that you are being selfless or that you have stopped obsessing over yourself; this gives you even more reason to continue to be an unselfish person.

5. **Ask yourself about what you want vs. what you need.** Selfish people are always repeating that mantra, "I want, I want, I want…" thinking that everything in the world should be theirs and that they should deserve every little thing that they dream about. Stop and ask yourself whether you really needed those five sweaters, or whether you really needed to choose the movie or restaurant when you were hanging out with your partner. If you dig deep enough, you will find that most of the things that you thought were necessary were quite easy to live without.

6. **Enjoy giving the spotlight to others.** Selfish people cringe when someone else goes in the spotlight because they always want it for themselves. If you want to stop being selfish, then you must not only give up the spotlight, but you must enjoy letting other people take it. Stop trying to be the bride at every wedding and let other brides have their time in the spotlight. Be proud of other people for achieving things instead of wishing it were you.

7. **Take in criticism.** People who are selfish are always thinking that their way of living life is best and that anyone who tries to give them feedback is just trying to do them harm or has ulterior motives. Sure, you cannot believe all the criticism that comes

your way, but if you focus enough, you might see that a lot of people are telling you the same thing.

8. **Make a gratitude list.** Make a habit of writing down all the things you are grateful for every Sunday or at least once a week. Take the time to think of every individual thing that makes your life great, and do not spend all your time focusing on the things you do not have, or the things you wish you had, or all the "If only" chants that can ruin your day and your life. Think of things that are going well for you, from your health to your plethora of friends, and feel happy about what you have got.

Apostle Paul in Romans 12:3 (New Living Translation) says this, "Don't think you are better than you really are. Be honest in your evaluation of yourselves."

To reiterate the point stated above, Jesus' response to the question of the Pharisees, "Why then did Moses command a man give his wife a certificate of divorce and send her away?" (Matthew 19:7). Jesus replied, "Moses permitted you to divorce your wives because your hearts were hard." (Matthew 19:8). *Jesus wants us to understand the relational difficulty a prideful and selfish (hard hearted) person puts another person into.*

Overcome the pride and selfishness and then, the entire relationship will change for the glorious- better!

1C. The Designer's Intent – "In the Beginning it Was Not So" *(verse 8b)*

"Why then did Moses command a man give his wife a certificate of divorce and send her away?" (Matthew 19:7).

As stated before, Jesus' response is important; "Moses permitted you to divorce your wives because your hearts were hard, *but "in the beginning, it was not so"* (Matthew 19:8).

When Jesus was questioned about divorce, he pointed back to the ideal established at the creation: "Haven't you read that at the beginning the Creator 'made them male and female' and said, "For this reason a man will leave his father and mother and be united to his wife, and the two will become one flesh"? (more detail on this provided in learned Lesson #7).

God had, and has, a plan for this unique "mystery" called marriage. In an online article, Dr. Richard Fisher, retired Professor of Biblical Studies at Moody Bible Institute, beautifully explains the "mystery" this way:

"The Apostle Paul referred to marriage as a "mystery" (Ephesians 5) because marriage is really a reminder of, a celebration of, and a commitment to God's plan and provision: (1) to restore the relationship between Himself, the man, and the woman, and (2) to re-form His intended partnership between the man, the woman, and Himself as we navigate our life adventures together to fulfill our destiny (Genesis 1:27-28)."

"In this way, marriage is more than an end in itself – it is a profound mystery, showcasing God's redemptive vision for our broken world. And that vision steps closer to ultimate consummation – one human couple at a time."

"And this is where the mystery comes into focus: *Marriage symbolizes the spiritual unity and special relationship God has for us as a couple (His image bearers) to have with Him.*"

Our purpose for this book is to explore seven key learnings from the Garden of Eden, which all provide more detail as to why Jesus pointed the religious leaders (Pharisees) of his day to the magnificent truths revealed in the beginning, that can heal and advance all marriage relationships.

Therefore, continue with us as we describe what the Designer (God) intended the marriage relationship to really be. Divorce was not the ideal option then nor the expectation. Unfortunately, it has become so in recent times, but in this book, we will discover why, *"in the beginning, it was not so."*

A Side Note:

Divorce and remarriage are particularly sensitive issues today. Nothing should be done to encourage or justify divorce. Yet those who have suffered the agony of marital breakup should not be treated with a Pharisee-like condemnation.

God has forgiveness for our sins and provides a mercy that can meet the needs of the divorced and make up for the sorrow involved in termination of a marriage.

The church must not legislate divorce or remarriage. It can only affirm the standards of Scripture, help those in difficulty to learn to express Christ's forgiveness within marriage, and – should sin shatter a home - offer love and support to the sufferers.

Now you are beginning to understand the profoundness of Jesus' response to the religious leaders of His time.

Hopefully, you also are beginning to clearly understand the premise of this book as stated in its title, *"In The Beginning It Was Not So"*.

CHAPTER 2

A Beautiful Beginning –
Life in the Garden

Genesis 2:8-15; 22,25; 3:8 (New Life Version)

⁸ The Lord God planted a garden to the east in Eden (related to a word meaning "luxurious"). He put the man there whom He had made. ⁹ And the Lord God made to grow out of the ground every tree that is pleasing to the eyes and good for food. And He made the tree of life grow in the center of the garden, and the tree of learning of good and bad.

¹⁰ Now a river flowed out of Eden to water the garden. And from there it divided and became four rivers. ¹¹ The name of the first is Pishon. It flows around the whole land of Havilah, where there is gold. ¹² The gold of that land is good. Bdellium and onyx stone are there. ¹³ The name of the second river is Gihon. It flows around the whole land of Cush. ¹⁴ The name of the third river is Tigris. It flows east of Assyria. And the fourth river is the Euphrates.

¹⁵ The Lord God took the man and put him in the Garden of Eden to work it and take care of it.

²² Then the Lord God made a woman from the rib he had taken out of the man, and he brought her to the man.

25 Adam and his wife were both naked, and they felt no shame.

3:8 Then the man and his wife heard the sound of the Lord God as he was walking in the garden in the cool of the day.

Throughout human history, the garden has symbolized a place of beauty, peace, and rest.

In biblical times, people from Mesopotamia to Egypt viewed gardens as places to relax in and enjoy. The author of Ecclesiastes "made gardens and parks and planted all kinds of fruit trees in them" (Ecclesiastes 2:5).

One of the three places where gardens play prominent roles in sacred history is the parklike Garden of Eden (Genesis 2:3). This is where Adam was placed and where he and Eve were united, disobeyed God, and were exiled from this paradise.

Symbolically, Eden has always represented the idyllic state, where beauty and peace reign.

The Garden of Eden (or some say the "Garden in Eden") was an ideal environment. There Adam was to cultivate and keep this enormous park, with all its goodly trees, abundant fruit crop, and four mighty rivers that flowed from Eden to other regions of the Near East.

In Ezekiel 28:13 and 31:9, Eden is referred to as "the Garden of God."

Many years ago, growing up in a little small neighborhood church, often you would hear, on any given Sunday, a soloist singing this incredibly old hymn referencing life in the Garden of Eden.

Inspired by the Gospel of John, chapter 20 [1-18], this hymn celebrates the joyous companionship its author, C. Austin Miles, experiences with Jesus as he walks through the Garden. (https://www.umcdiscipleship.org/resources/history-of-hymns-i-come-to-the-garden-alone)

The lyrics were as follows:

In the Garden

I come to the garden alone,
While the dew is still on the roses,
And the voice I hear falling on my ear,
The Son of God discloses...

And He walks with me, and He talks with me,
And He tells me I am His own,
And the joy we share as we tarry there,
None other, has ever, known!

He speaks and the sound of His voice,
Is so sweet the birds hush their singing,
And the melody that he gave to me,
Within my heart is ringing . . .

And He walks with me, and He talks with me,
And He tells me I am His own,
And the joy we share as we tarry there,
None other, has ever, known!
And the joy we share as we tarry there,
None other, has ever, known!

Words and Music by C. Austin Miles, 1912

This hymn provides an imaginary glimpse of what life could have been like for Adam (and Eve) in the Garden of Eden. This beautiful place of vibrant flowers, lush greenery, fruitful trees, birds chirping, where peace and tranquility abound.

"He walks with me and talks with me" just warms the heart knowing that in the beginning, God enjoyed intimate relationship with the man and woman He created. The hymn speaks of where intimate conversation was shared, quality time was enjoyed, and the time spent produced a feeling of immense joy. Joy like "none other has ever known!"

Obviously, the "ever known" reference is more an expression of the songwriter, than that of the first family. For Adam and Eve, this was the ONLY kind of relationship like this ever known! But think of that, to have that kind of daily intimate connection and relationship with the Creator of the Universe; to enjoy a life with Him that produces rest, peace, and joy-how awesome would that be!

Well, we too, can experience such a relationship with Him even today. As a matter of fact, God wants that kind of relationship with us. In Revelation 3:20, God says He "stands at the door (of our hearts) and knocks". If we open our hearts (the door), He will "come in and eat with us, and we with Him." The reference to eating is all about communion, community, relationship building, and developing intimacy.

We can, in essence, experience a similar joy of relationship in our "Garden", alone with God, where He speaks to us, and we speak with Him. Let us take advantage of that opportunity daily!

But what about the relationship that this first man and woman enjoyed *together*? There are a few things we can surmise about their relationship from what we read in the book of Genesis.

First, they were together. This is obvious from the fact that the Bible speaks of them being in the Garden together. However, being in the same physical location does not result in oneness in your relationship. The marriage relationship is a unique one. It requires more of us than we initially imagine. As a result, it is imperative to "leave" others, to focus on building life and love together. We will discuss that further as we explore *"Your path to oneness"* in learned Lesson #7.

Second, they were united. Webster's definition of the word *unite* is, to couple; to cause to adhere; to attach; to incorporate in one; to ally; and to join in interest or affection. "Uniting" is the one thing that can make a marriage relationship one that thrives, and not one that just survives. Why? Because your spouse must take the highest place of honor, respect, and admiration in your life, excepting only to your relationship with God. This only happens when the "two become one". Again, we will go deeper into this "uniting" together concept in learned Lesson #7.

Third, they were naked, and not ashamed (Genesis 2:25). Being "naked and not ashamed" is so enthralling, so profound, and so enlightening that if you can grasp the depth of meaning of this concept, and can apply the principles to your marriage, it will transform your marriage from mediocre to magnificent seemingly overnight!

You will read the explanation and broader impact of this point later in learned Lesson #7 (but do not skip ahead, or you will miss all the other great stuff in between!). But to whet your appetite, just know that the impact of being "naked and not ashamed" goes far deeper than the amount of clothing you choose or not choose to wear. This "nakedness" is what produces intimacy in the marriage relationship. Stay tuned!

The love story in Eden began with Adam and Eve enjoying bone-of-my-bones, flesh-of-my-flesh intimacy. But the same two people who were naked and unashamed are, only a few verses later, trying to cover up their shame. The same husband who held out his hand to his wife to welcome her, exclaiming, "At last!" only a few verses later point the finger of blame in her direction, saying, "The woman whom you gave to be with me, she gave me fruit of the tree, and I ate." (Genesis 3:12).

This partnership that was intended to bless the world brought a curse upon the world. But the purpose of this book is not to focus on the sin that cursed the symbolic idyllic state, where beauty and peace reigned (The Garden of Eden), but to focus our attention on the explicit lessons to be learned from the first couple's life in this very same Garden.

Perhaps the next edition of this work will look at the seven not-so-positive lessons learned from the Garden that caused the first couple's relationship to dramatically change. We can always learn from the mistakes of others.

But remember this, ever since this first marriage went so terribly wrong, God has been working out his plan to present a perfected bride to the perfect groom. This speaks of His people (the bride) learning how to become the perfect bride for Jesus Christ (the Groom).

The human marriage covenant relationship is designed to be a representation of the beautiful mystery of God's ultimate spiritual relationship with us.

Let us learn how to be that perfected bride to a perfectly awesome groom—both naturally and spiritually!

Seven Marriage Lessons Learned in the Garden (Genesis 2:15-24):

The following scripture in Genesis 2 provides the backdrop for the lessons learned from this beautiful place we call, *The Garden of Eden.*

Genesis 2:15-24 (New International Version)
(parentheses added)

> *15 The Lord God took the man and put him in the Garden of Eden to work it and take care of it.* **(Lesson 1)** *16 And the Lord God commanded the man, "You are free to eat from any tree in the garden; 17 but you must not eat from the tree of the knowledge of good and evil,* **(Lesson 2)** *for when you eat from it you will certainly die."*
>
> *18 The Lord God said, "It is not good for the man to be alone.* **(Lesson 3)** *I will make a helper suitable for him." (a companion for him, a perfectly suited partner).* **(Lesson 4)**
>
> *19 Now the Lord God had formed out of the ground all the wild animals and all the birds in the sky. He brought them to the man to see what he would name them; and whatever the man called each living creature, that was its name. 20 So the man gave names to all the livestock, the birds in the sky and all the wild animals. But for Adam no suitable helper was found.*
>
> *21 So the Lord God caused the man to fall into a deep sleep; and while he was sleeping, he took one of the man's ribs and then closed up the place with flesh. 22*

Then the Lord God made a woman from the rib he had taken out of the man, and he brought her to the man. **(Lesson 5)**

²³ *(Excited Voice) At last! a suitable companion, a perfect partner! Bone from my bones. Flesh from my flesh. I will call this one "woman" as an eternal reminder that she was taken out of man.* **(Lesson 6)**

²⁴ *That is why a man leaves his father and mother and is united to his wife, and they become one flesh.* **(Lesson 7)**

We go now to this beautiful Garden of Eden where God puts to work the man he created, for a purpose! Our learned Lesson #1.

CHAPTER 3

Lesson 1: Every Man has a Purpose – *Find Yours (Genesis 2:15)*

"The Lord God took the man and put him in the Garden of Eden to work it and take care of it."

Adam had been given the responsibility of pruning, harvesting fruit, and keeping the ground free of brush and undergrowth for a long time in this beautiful paradise of Eden.

Then God gave Adam a major assignment in natural history. He was given the task to classify and name every species of animal and bird found in the Garden.

With its mighty rivers and broad expanse, the garden must have had hundreds of species of mammal, reptile, insect, and bird, to say nothing of the flying insects.

It is said that it took the Swedish scientist Linnaeus several decades to classify all species known to European scientists in the eighteenth century. Doubtless there were considerably more by that time than in Adam's day; and, of course, the range of fauna in Eden may have been more limited than those available to Linnaeus.

But at the same time, it must have taken a good deal of study for Adam to examine each specimen and decide on an appropriate name for it, especially since he had absolutely no human tradition behind him, so far as nomenclature was concerned.

It must have required some years, or, at the very least, a considerable number of months for him to complete this comprehensive inventory of all the birds, beasts, and insects that populated the Garden of Eden.

Note that man's task was *to care for and maintain* the trees of the garden. Not until after the fall, when he is condemned to cultivate the soil, does this task change. Stay true to your purpose.

There is something significant about finding our purpose. How many times have you asked yourself, "what am I doing here?", or "what *is* my purpose?" Purpose gives us, well, purpose. It gives us meaning and significance. Many people identify themselves by the vocation or advocation they undertake. But those choices identify us based on what we do, which causes us to live our lives and gain our self-satisfaction based on performance. Is that all there is to finding our purpose, simply by finding the right job or hobby?

Rick Warren in his popular book, The Purpose Driven Life, states that "being successful and fulfilling your life's purpose are *not at all* the same issue!" He goes on to say, "You could reach all your personal goals, becoming a raving success by the world's standard, and *still* miss the purposes for which God created you. You need more than self-help advice."

Rick Warren's point is that we find our purpose when we become what God has created us to be. But how do we discover the purpose for which we were created? Warren goes on to state that you have two options:

1. *Speculation* – this is the option Warren says most people choose. When people say, "I've always thought life is…, "they mean, 'This is the best guess I can come up with.'"

Perhaps one method of "speculation" is provided by John Robson, Higher Awareness, Inc., who states that "I am deeply committed to helping people to change, grow, be more productive and create more magic and miracles in their lives. I want to empower others to trust themselves and use their own natural thinking and intuitive abilities so they can get out of their ruts and lead more meaningful, joyful, and purposeful lives."

"I believe we each have the answers to the questions of our life inside of us. We need only learn how to draw them out."

The answers to the questions of our life are inside of us? What answers? What questions? Do you have any idea how to mine these intrinsic answers? Do you even have any idea of the right questions to ask to discover your purpose? Most of us do not.

John Robson does provide a list of questions asked in a questionnaire that when completed will, he suggests, provide insight into your possible purpose in life. Perhaps one flaw in that is that the "answer" will be self-directed based on what I believe the answers to be—more speculative perhaps, yet it does provide some guidance for you.

Oh yes, for the curious among us, here is the list of questions Robson provides for you to answer:

1. What do you sense might be your true vocation or service?

2. What is your most joyous and meaningful activity?

3. What is your heart's desire?

4. How do you experience selflessness?

5. What is your true guidance?

6. What do you hold sacred in your life?

7. What are your highest virtues?

2. *Revelation* – Per Rick Warren there is an alternative to speculation about the meaning and purpose for life. It is revelation. We can turn to what God has revealed about life in his Word. He says, "the easiest way to discover the purpose of an invention is to ask the creator of it. The same is true for discovering your life's purpose: Ask God."

Connected to the "revelation" option is the point that God is not just the starting point of your life; he is the *source* of it.

Ephesians 1:11 (The Message) gives three insights into your purpose:

1. You discover your identity and purpose through a relationship with Jesus Christ. The more you know and understand Him, the better you will know yourself, and your purpose.

2. God's purpose for your life predates your conception. God was thinking of you long before you ever thought about him. Warren states the broader point so masterfully: "you may choose your career, your spouse, your hobbies, and many other parts of your life, but you don't get to choose your purpose."

3. The purpose of your life fits into a much larger, cosmic purpose that God has designed for eternity.

I can attest to the wonder of this "revelation" approach to finding your purpose in life. For years I thought my purpose was to become a corporate leader, managing, training, and developing other leaders. Yet, as the years progressed and my relationship with God matured, I began developing a greater interest in leading couples through their marriage difficulties, even while still working in corporate America.

It was not until going through the particularly challenging time of separation, divorce, personal spiritual growth, and then remarriage, that I began to fully understand, embrace, and become fully focused on my "purpose" (some say "my calling"). I realized my calling is leading, counseling, coaching, mentoring, training, and encouraging married (and pre-married) couples. And now after over 25 years of preparation, I am now partnering with my lovely bride of nearly 15 years, retired from corporate America, spending countless hours ministering to couples, and now writing a book! Who would have thought this would be my purpose in life! But God knew all along.

Life Purpose is NOT a job description. It focuses more on quali-ties and the journey, not the destination.

Let us return to the Garden of Eden where we can see these "revelation" principles unfold. We observe that man's task was *to care for and maintain* the trees of the garden. This first man (Adam) was given an exceptionally large but specific task. Notice that Adam knew what his assigned purpose was (to care for and maintain the garden). Adam did not have to wonder about it, pray about it, or figure something out. Adam's purpose was "revealed" to him.

You would think that Adam would have complained about all he had to do in caring for all the trees in the Garden. After all, this was an immense area with a large number and variety of trees. Not to mention the number of flowers, and plants, and other such garden variety items. But nowhere was it written that Adam complained about what he was told to do, because of the relationship he had with the one directing him (God). That relationship was one of complete trust and total obedience. If God said it, then Adam did it.

Oh, but if we too, could all have that kind of trust in the words of our Father!

To further the plan God had for Adam, he gave him an additional assignment. God told Adam to name all the animals that God had made. The scripture says, "So the man gave names to all the livestock, the birds in the sky and all the wild animals."

You might wonder, why would God add to what was already a monumental task of maintaining this vast acreage of trees and flowers, etc., that were in the Garden? It is in times like these that we must trust God in the process of developing *in us* the skills, experience, and mindset (or heart-set) we need to fulfill the purposes He has *for* us.

Remember, **God knows what he is doing, even when we do not understand.**

A few principles learned about purpose:

Recall what was stated previously when discussing the insights about your purpose, in that the purpose of your life fits into a much larger, cosmic purpose that God has designed for eternity.

There was purpose in what God instructed Adam to do. To that end, here are a few principles gleaned from Adam's experience in the Garden:

1. In fulfilling his purpose, Adam demonstrated **TRUST**.

Did you ever wonder whether Adam asked God "why", when God said to care for and maintain the entire Garden, and then name all the animals? Wouldn't you look at the enormity of the assignment, recognizing that YOU had to do all this all by yourself, want to ask God, "couldn't you just make a few more of me so I can have some help here?"

Okay, I know that is anti-spiritual and all, but practically speaking, wouldn't you say that was a lot for one man to do all by himself? Yet nowhere is it written that Adam questioned the purposes of God or the plan of God in the process. Now that is TRUST!

Of course, Adam had no reason not to trust the words of God, because those were the *only* words he heard! Today our ears, minds, and hearts are bombarded with countermanding commands, demands, and voices that often muffle the small still voice of God.

These distracting "noises" can cause us to doubt (or not to trust) God's word to us—words that are only given to help us to do what God has purposed us to do.

There is something to be said about taking time to get away from the "noise" of the many "voices", for the opportunity to only hear the loving sound of God's still, quiet, reassuring voice.

You can trust Him.

2. In fulfilling his purpose Adam demonstrated **OBEDIENCE**.

Adam (and all mankind) was created with a heart to obey God's commands. He had not yet been presented a different option from which to choose not to obey. (That comes in Genesis 3 - not our focus for this book).

Of course, today, man (i.e., mankind), must <u>learn</u> to obey and walk in obedience to God's commands. But how do we learn obedience? Through your relationship with someone with whom you develop respect. Out of a heart of respect for that person, you are then willing to do what they ask of you. So, it is with God.

As our relationship with God develops (by getting to know Him through praying; Bible reading and teaching; worship; through our daily experiences and circumstances; and through a community of believers), we learn to believe in what he says, and to respect him for his love and care for us. From this heart-connected relationship, we learn to walk in obedience to the One we have learned knows much more than us.

Man (mankind) was created (and still has that internal ability) to trust and walk in obedience.

3. In fulfilling his purpose Adam demonstrated the importance of having **PURPOSE**.

Imagine if you would, Adam sitting around all day, having nothing to do, having no responsibilities at all, doing nothing but walking around the Garden all day waiting for God to show up for their evening talk. That does not sound like a very purposeful life now does it.

But God in his preeminence, created purpose **for** Adam, to produce purpose **in** Adam.

Wow! Did you catch that? God created an opportunity in the Garden for Adam to work and labor, on purpose, for a purpose.

Having to work in the Garden to care for and maintain it, and name the animals (which were many), must have been a full-time job. This provided something meaningful for Adam to do, which gave him purpose (meaningful work to do).

In the fulfillment of his purpose (doing the work), Adam learned how satisfying it was to complete the assignments God gave to him. This made Adam feel good about himself (self-worth), knowing how pleased God would be with him (feeling appreciated and valued).

These feelings that Adam (man) derived from meaningful work, would be intrinsic character traits Adam would need for his future.

All healthy and mature Men, (not to exclude the women), are created with the internal need to find fulfillment in their work. This impacts their view of themselves and of their own self-worth. God created purpose **for** Adam (work), to produce purpose **in** Adam (value and self-worth). So good!

But get this next point!

4. God's broader plan for Adam was for him to use his purpose to **PREPARE** for his promise!

If you notice in Genesis 2:18, God said it was *"not good for man to be alone."* (more on that in learned Lesson #3), *"I will make a helper suitable for him."* (more on that in learned Lesson #4).

Then in verses 19 and 20 it says, *"Now the Lord God had formed out of the ground all the wild animals and all the birds in the sky. He brought them to the man to see what he would name them; and whatever the man called each living creature, that was its name. ²⁰ So the man gave names to all the livestock, the birds in* *the sky and all the wild animals. <u>But for Adam no suitable helper was found</u>."*

But for Adam no suitable helper was found. God promised to make a helper suitable for Adam in verse 18. Accordingly, God used the responsibility he gave to Adam to name the animals, to determine if the "helper" he wanted for Adam was among that group of other creatures. From that experience God determined for Adam "no suitable helper was found" (among them).

When God discovered among all the creatures named that still "no suitable helper was found", he created a different kind of "creature" (one suitable for him) and brought her to Adam. But catch this! By having Adam interacting and naming the animals, *Adam learned how to distinguish one creature from another, and recognize their distinctiveness.* That is why he was able to recognize that this last "creature" presented to him was nothing like these others! He declared with amazed excitement, "this is bone of my bones and flesh of my flesh. I'll call her woman because she was taken from man (himself!)."

Adam was able to distinguish his new bride (the one more "suitable" for him), from the other creatures, because of the purpose God had given him beforehand to interact with and to name them.

God used Adam's purpose (naming the creatures) to prepare him for his promise (the unique creature – his woman!).

Yet there is a deeper application to this idea of using His purpose to prepare man for his promise. As we talk about the fulfilment that comes from finding and fulfilling your purpose, there is a relational aspect to this process as well.

It is widely understood by psychologists, therapists, and other professionals in human self-actualization that the more positive view we have of ourselves, the better able we are to give ourselves to others in relationship.

Our personal perspective of who we are, our self-worth or self-value, is an essential component of our self-awareness. Knowing who you are, and feeling good about who you are, enables us to be more unselfish, more giving, and more aware of the needs of others. Each of these positive traits are healthy attributes for healthy relationships.

But knowing "the real you", is much more than just being based on what you do. We all have that "real you" living deep inside of us that is a truthful representation of who we really are, our "genuine selves", you might say.

Knowing ourselves for who we really are, and feeling good about who we are, is the essence of self-awareness which comes from understanding who God made you to be. That awareness is then validated by the way we live out our lives as demonstrated by what we ultimately do, and how we feel about what we do.

That "do" can be a fulfilling vocational career that provides the ability for you to "do you" in a productive and rewarding manner. It can be an advocation consisting of service to others, or a life of philanthropy that comes from a heart to give to others and help them in ways where they are unable to help themselves.

The key is to *find that purpose, live that purpose, and feel the internal reward that comes from such fulfillment.*

Why is this so important? When a man feels good about himself, he will not have to seek that fulfillment from another person. If you do, the relationship with that person then becomes a focus on what you can "get" from the relationship (self-worth), which is a selfish pursuit; rather than what you can "give" to that person (your real self), which is from where real love and loving emanates.

Do you naturally feel good about yourself, or do you prefer others to tell you that you have done a good job? Do you seek fame and glory, or do you have confidence in your life despite others not knowing about your successes? Depending on your answers your self-esteem might be based on what others say about you more than what you say about yourself.

Having positive feelings about yourself is necessary for your overall emotional health and well-being. Without properly meeting esteem needs, we are filled with feelings of inferiority and negativity regarding our lives.

This was the other important aspect of God using Adam's completion of meaningful work (purpose) to fulfill his promise. When completing his work, Adam learned to value himself and feel good about himself, in preparation for the relationship he was to have with his future companion.

Find your purpose and fulfill your purpose. In so doing you will then feel good about yourself and your value. Then you can freely give yourself to that one God has promised to you. That is another way God uses your purpose to prepare you for your promise!

In summary-the significance of finding your purpose:

To finish up this learned Lesson #1 – Every Man has a Purpose- *Find Yours*, let us summarize what we have discussed.

1. We are created on purpose, with purpose. Find your meaningful vocation or advocation, then do it and do it well!

2. God has instilled purpose within each of us – to have meaning, value, and self-worth.

3. God uses His purpose for us (to *do* something–work, etc.); to develop purpose in us (to *be* something–person with confidence and self-worth).

4. It is through our relationship with God that gives us the ability to discover our "revealed" purpose. Maturity is "revealed" purpose.

5. It is imperative that we know our purpose and walk in obedience to Him who gave us our purpose, to enjoy the fulfilling life for which God created us.

6. When we are fulfilling our purpose (both meaningful work and the feeling of self-worth/value), the promised help and helper will be provided.

7. Fulfilling our purpose adds to our sense of meaning and self-worth, which we need to feel better about ourselves in our relationship with another. Absent of such can cause us to look to another person to fulfill that part in us.

CHAPTER 4

Lesson 2: With Freedom comes Boundaries – *For our Good (Genesis 2:16, 17)*

"And the Lord God commanded the man, you are free to eat from any tree in the garden; But from the tree of knowledge of good and evil you shall not eat, for in the day you eat from it you shall surely die." (NASB).

Adam is brought into covenant relationship with God, who grants him permission to eat the fruit of every tree in the garden except one: the tree of the knowledge of good and evil.

Genesis 2:16 is the first time in the Bible that the verb meaning "to command" appears. Whatever the man had to do in the garden, the focus of the narrative is on keeping God's commandments. God created humans with the capacity to obey him and then tested them with commands.

One view of the "knowledge of good and evil" is the capacity to discern between moral good and evil. It may well be a Hebrew idiom standing for the full range of moral knowledge represented by the two extremes. To eat of the tree of the knowledge of good and evil will therefore make man like God.

The context in Genesis 3:6 suggests the tree's fruit gives one wisdom "capable of making one wise", which certainly includes the capacity to discern between good and evil (or right and wrong). Note, however, that this capacity does not include the ability to _do_ what is right.

Adam and Eve yielded to temptation and partook of the forbidden fruit. They certainly did not drop dead on that fateful day. But the death that overtook the guilty pair that day was spiritual only; (physical death did not come until centuries later.) (Genesis 5:5).

From that moment on, Adam and Eve fell into a state of spiritual death, separated from the living God through their violation of His covenant.

It is this aspect of death (spiritual) that overtook our first parents immediately upon their act of sin (disobedience).

Consequences of disobedience –

God prohibits man from eating of the tree. The prohibition becomes as a test to see if man will be satisfied with his role and place, or if he will try to ascend to the divine level.

This is the reason for God's "do not eat from the tree of the knowledge of good and evil" command. **It was for Adam and Eve's good, not to harm them or limit them**. Yet consequently, not only was there immediate spiritual death, broken relationship, and sin, they now would no longer remain in a state of innocence, but have personal knowledge of the moral law, with the capacity to discern good from evil (Genesis 3:22).

They now had a (guilty) personal experience of evil and the internal emotional struggle that moral awareness brings. But now being morally corrupted and rebellious would cause them not to choose what is right. Their morally corrupted heart was now different than what they had before disobedience. Now things had changed internally with Adam and Eve (the world's first parents).

A Side Note:

This internal confliction and emotional struggle inherited by man's sin, (the first parents), was centuries later described by the Apostle Paul in Romans 7:19 when he said, "I do not do the good I want, but the evil I do not want is what I keep on doing."

This is a present-day internal struggle we still all wrestle with. *The knowledge of what is right or wrong, without the desire to DO what is right instead of wrong, brings internal turmoil and frustration.*

Thankfully, Paul realized the solution for us all: "Who will deliver me from this body of death? Thanks be to God through Jesus Christ our Lord!" (Romans 7:24b, 25a).

There were other consequences for them eating from the tree of knowledge of good and evil:

1. It was apparent from their attitude of "guilty fear" toward God (Genesis 3:10), that alienation toward God was shown by their vain attempt to hide from Him when he came to have fellowship (or companionship) with them in the cool of the evening (Genesis 3:8). The trusting and intimate relationship they had with God was forever changed.

2. Then there was expulsion from the Garden of Eden itself (where they had enjoyed intimate and cordial fellowship with God). God knew at this point that they must be banned from

the garden so that they would not be able to achieve their goal of being godlike and thus live forever, (after eating of the fruit from the tree of life), a divine characteristic (Genesis 3:24).

3. Another consequence was toil and pain for both in the eking out of a living from the soil (Adam/Man), and in the process of childbirth (Eve/Woman). The once simple purpose of taking care of the beautiful Garden, man would now have to toil and labor to create beauty for himself.

Woman would now experience the "pain of labor" through childbirth.

What was once easily provided for man and woman, is now that which we must labor for.

4. Another consequence was the eventual death of the body and its reversion to the soil from which it was made-Ashes to ashes; Dust to dust. (Genesis 3:16-19, 23-24).

There will be a time for man to possess moral discernment/ wisdom, as God reveals and imparts it to him, but it is not something to be grasped at to become "a god." In fact, the command to be obedient was the first lesson in moral discernment/wisdom. God was essentially saying: "Here is lesson one– respect my authority and commands. Disobey me and you will die."

When man disobeys, he decides he does not want to acquire moral wisdom God's way, but instead tries to rise immediately to the divine level. Of course, today that decision still brings consequences.

Why boundaries are beneficial

Our actions have consequences. Unfortunately, many times the consequences of our actions are only realized after we have acted. Wouldn't it be great to know what the consequences will be for our actions long before we decide on that specific action? That is not always likely.

Therefore, there was the boundary established for Adam and Eve ("do not eat of the tree of knowledge of good and evil"). Although we may not understand why, we must trust God's wisdom and accept that He has our best interest in mind when he tells us "don't do that!" His commands are to protect us, not to limit our freedom, or control our behavior.

Also, in our personal relationships we must establish boundaries.

The following definitions and descriptions of boundaries were posted online by *The Resilience Centre*, by Ida Soghomonian.

She stated:

A Boundary is anything that marks a border or the limits of an area, a dividing line. It is a real or imagined line that marks the edge or the limit of a subject, principle, or relationship.

Personal boundaries are guidelines, rules, or limits that a person creates to identify reasonable, safe, and permissible ways for other people to behave toward them and how they will respond when someone passes those limits.

Boundaries are essential to healthy relationships.

Boundaries draw a clear line around what is okay for us and what is not.

Boundaries are important for both individuals in a relationship, and for the health of the relationship itself. Without clear boundaries, we may feel resentful, taken advantage of and eventually shut down and withdraw.

Clear boundaries allow us to remain connected and communicating these boundaries shows our respect for the relationship.

Setting clear personal boundaries is key to ensuring relationships are mutually respectful, supportive, and caring.

Establishing healthy boundaries

Establishing healthy boundaries in a relationship allows both partners to feel comfortable and develop positive self-esteem. To establish boundaries, you need to be clear with your partner who you are, what you want, your beliefs and values, and your limits.

A lot of times, we tend to focus on adjusting to others, taking time away from focusing on ourselves. Setting boundaries for yourself that reflect who you are and who you ultimately want to be will only enhance setting boundaries with your partner in a relationship.

Joaquín Selva, Bc.S., Psychologist, (with a focus on behavioral neuroscience), suggests the following tips for establishing boundaries with your partner in your relationship:

1. Examine the boundaries that already exist

The first part of setting boundaries is examining the boundaries that already exist (or are lacking) in one's life. For example, a woman might decide that she has healthy boundaries with her romantic partner, but not with her friends and coworkers. From there, she can decide what types of boundaries she wants to set with her friends and coworkers.

2. Say no simply but firmly

As for how to exactly set these boundaries, "Say 'no' simply but firmly to something you do not want to do. Do not feel that you need to explain." Not overexplaining is a crucial aspect of setting boundaries, as everyone has the right to determine what they do and do not want to do.

3. Keep the focus on yourself

This brings up another important point: Keep the focus on yourself. Instead of setting a boundary by saying something like, "You have to stop bothering me after work", a person can say, "I need some time to myself when I get back from work."

4. Set boundaries with consequences

Another important thing to remember is: It is impossible to set boundaries without setting consequences. This means that when setting boundaries, it is important to explicitly state why they are important.

For example, a person in an unhealthy relationship might declare that his partner needs to start respecting his career goals if his partner wants to continue being in a relationship with him. It is also crucial to only declare consequences that one is willing to follow through on, or else the boundaries will not be effective.

In general, the key to setting boundaries is first figuring out what you want from your various relationships, setting boundaries based on those desires, and then being clear with yourself and with other people about your boundaries.

Setting and establishing healthy boundaries is a skill, and it takes time! Remember, healthy boundaries do not come easy, but if you trust your instincts, be open, and practice with your partner, the relationship will only get stronger over time.

If you break your own boundaries because you fear your partner's reaction, that is a HUGE red flag. In a healthy relationship, you should never feel afraid of your partner or their reactions.

Why Boundaries in Marriage Are Good for Your Relationship

Marriage is an undertaking for adults who are mature enough to handle the relationship dynamics.

Theoretically, a marriage is about two people sharing everything with each other; however, realistically, statistics show that when boundaries in marriage are absent, the marriage probably will not last.

1. Emotional Boundaries Strengthen the Emotional Connection in a Marriage

Emotional connection is the most important pillar in a marriage because it is the foundation of a genuine relationship. But what is emotional connection?

Well, emotional connection refers to authentic love experienced in a marriage. For example, you appreciate each other; have many shared experiences in life; and you try your best not to hurt each other's feelings.

Contrary to popular belief, the best way to strengthen the emotional connection in a marriage is not experiencing all life has to offer with each other. The fact is that emotional boundaries are essential in every sustainable marriage. Let me explain.

Let us say you love your spouse so much that you are together 24/7 and you never give each other any space. This marriage will eventually have a suffocating effect on either or both partners which will lead to arguments.

A couple setting emotional boundaries in a marriage will give each other some space. Which gives you both an opportunity to observe how wonderful your spouse is from a distance. As a result, you get to appreciate each other even more. Emotional boundaries such as this will strengthen the emotional connection in your marriage.

2. Physical Boundaries Improve the Quality of Intimacy in a Marriage

While having your own interests is paramount in maintaining and building attraction in your relationship, many marriages fail due to miscommunication and intimacy problems in the bedroom.

Sexual intimacy is not something that most couples discuss prior to marriage and this can cause problems when a couple's sexual preferences are mismatched.

There are no hard and fast rules here (pardon the pun) other than it is important not to get your sex education from porn which can result in unrealistic expectations and a lack of true intimacy.

Hence, setting physical boundaries around intimacy can be paramount in your marriage. But what does that mean?

Setting physical boundaries in marriage means you communicate to your partner what you like and what you do not like, so your partner does not have to go through a process of elimination or feel frustrated that they seem unable to fulfill you.

3. Boundaries in Marriage Help You Stress Less

The most stress and anxiety come from trying to control what is outside of your control. For example, trying to control your partner makes you become stressed and anxious and alienates your partner.

In other words, a marriage without boundaries leads to controlling behaviors which cause stress and anxiety for all concerned. Thus, you need to understand what is under your control and what is outside your control in your marriage. All *your* actions are under your control – or they should be.

While you cannot control your spouse's behavior, you most certainly can influence it. The best way to influence your spouse is to be the best version of yourself. This naturally encourages your partner to match your effort.

4. Boundaries in Marriage Add More Fun to Your Life

When you allow some space in your marriage, you can stay flirtatious and continually increase attraction between you and your spouse forever. Never stop seducing your spouse and you can both enjoy the fun that comes with creating a great marriage!

The art of seduction is a journey rather than a destination. Keep creating fun moments along your journey!

5. Boundaries in Marriage Give You Opportunities to Grow Together

Because you have set boundaries in marriage, you both have more flexibility which allows you to adjust according to different situations in life. As a result, you and your spouse will be well-calibrated and can grow together in harmony in the long run.

Although you have the freedom to live life as you want in becoming an adult, it is imperative that we follow the advice the Apostle Paul gave to the church at Galatia when he told them, "So don't use your freedom as an excuse to do anything you want." (Galatians 5:13b – Contemporary English Version).

We must establish boundaries in our marriage relationship as part of our love for, and covenant commitment to, each other.

Some examples of healthy boundaries:

Personal boundaries – to address your unhealthy habit of watching pornography, you decide to monitor more closely what you watch on TV or view on the internet; you avoid late-late-night solo internet surfing; you establish accountability partners.

Social boundaries – to guard your heart and avoid unhealthy attention from and attraction to people of the opposite sex, you agree with your spouse not to maintain close personal ties with men or women of the opposite sex where you spend an inordinate amount of alone time with them physically or via social media.

Physical boundaries – as a recovering alcoholic or drug abuser you decide to go back no longer to bars, clubs, restaurants, or certain homes where you used to visit when engaging in past unhealthy activities. You also decide that you will no longer hang around those same people who are still actively involved with the vices from which you have recovered.

There are many more ways you can establish healthy boundaries for yourself and your marriage relationship. These are just a few examples.

The point is that these boundaries are for your good and for the good of your marriage. They are not to take the fun out of your life; but to put joy, fulfillment, and personal satisfaction into your life. There is great satisfaction in knowing you are making that personal sacrifice for the good of your spouse and in honor of the covenant commitment to the vows you made.

In summary-the significance of boundaries:

To finish up this learned Lesson #2 - With Freedom comes Boundaries - *For our Good*, let us summarize what we have discussed:

1. In the Garden there was tremendous freedom for Adam and Eve ("you are free to eat of every tree of the garden").

2. The one specific command ("but do not eat of the tree of knowledge of good and evil") was a boundary established for their good, to avoid the devastating consequences ("you will surely die").

3. For Adam and Eve the boundary established by God's command served to determine the degree of continual obedience and trust Adam and Eve had in their relationship with God. Our obedience to God's commands today also demonstrates the degree of trust we have in Him and our relationship with Him.

4. In our relationships with one another, boundaries serve as indicators of the degree of trust, respect, and appreciation we have for each other.

5. Boundaries in relationships must be established to enhance the emotional, physical, and spiritual intimacy of the relationship.

6. Setting clear personal boundaries is key to ensuring relationships are mutually respectful, supportive, and caring.

7. We must establish boundaries in our marriage relationship as part of our love for, and covenant commitment to, each other.

CHAPTER 5

Lesson 3: It's Not Good to Be Alone – *Man's Deepest Need Identified (Genesis 2:18a)*

"Then the Lord God said, *"It's not good for the man to be alone".*

Adam had been diligently occupied in his responsible task of pruning, harvesting fruit, and keeping the ground free of brush and undergrowth for a long time in this beautiful paradise of Eden. Perhaps God recognized that Adam had begun to feel a certain lonesomeness and inward dissatisfaction.

To compensate for this lonesomeness, God gave Adam a major assignment in natural history. He was given the task to classify and name every species of animal and bird found in the Garden.

With its mighty rivers and broad expanse, the garden must have had hundreds of species of mammal, reptile, insect, and bird, to say nothing of the flying insects.

Finally, after this assignment with all its absorbing interest had been completed, Adam perhaps felt a renewed sense of emptiness. Genesis 2:20 ends with the words "but for Adam no suitable helper was found."

God recognized Adam's foreseen need of companionship was not satisfied by the fellowship with the animals and birds (vv. 19-20).

After this long and unsatisfying experience as a lonely bachelor, God saw that Adam was emotionally prepared for a companion - a "suitable helper."

In our next learned lesson (Lesson #4), we will discuss what is meant by a "suitable helper". For this lesson let us take a deeper look at this need God recognized Adam had, even before Adam recognized it himself.

As stated above, God gave Adam a major assignment. He was given the task to classify and name every species of animal and bird found in the Garden. But notice this was after God had already said in Genesis 2:18 that, "It is not good for the man to be alone."

What do you mean alone! He had tons of animals, birds, insects, and other creatures around him all day, every day! You would think, after months of naming all these creatures and then using some of them to help maintain the Garden and till the soil, that having some "alone time" might just be what Adam needed!

But God recognized that Adam's need being met was not not con-tingent on having creatures around him or not, but that Adam had begun to feel a certain aloneness and inward discontent.

God understood Adam's innate need for companionship.

After all, each of the creatures that Adam spent tremendous time with naming them and interacting with, all had mates of the same nature, form, and habits ("after their kind"). But Adam alone had no companion.

In the Jamieson, Fausset & Brown Bible Commentary, it points out an additional thought of note from this scene. "In giving names to them he (Adam) *(parentheses added)* was led to exercise his powers of speech and to prepare for social intercourse with his partner, a creature yet to be formed."

Yes, God was working out his plan to address the need He earlier identified, that it was "not good for man to be alone." Adam needed what the other creatures already had, companionship with a creature "after his kind."

In college Psychology 101 classes many years ago, I was introduced to Maslow's hierarchy of needs. Maslow's hierarchy of needs is a motivational theory in psychology comprising of a five-tier model of human needs, often depicted as hierarchical levels within a pyramid. From the bottom of the hierarchy upwards, the needs are physiological (food and clothing), safety (security), love and belonging needs (friendship), esteem, and self-actualization.

For our purposes we will take a closer look at the third level of human needs (love and belonging). Our goal is not to dissect Maslow's theory, but to use it to gain greater insight into this need God so acutely recognized Adam had. It is essential for us that this need be met, to be able to enjoy mutually satisfying marriage relationships.

Love and belonging needs

After physiological and safety needs have been fulfilled, the third level of human needs is social and involves feelings of belongingness. The theory is that the need for interpersonal relationships motivates behavior. These social needs relate to human interaction. Examples include friendship, intimacy, trust, and acceptance, receiving and giving affection and love. Also among these needs are friendships and family bonds—both with biological family (parents, siblings, children) and chosen family (spouses and partners).

Physical and emotional intimacy ranging from sexual relationships to intimate emotional bonds are important to achieving a feeling of elevated kinship.

Humans are social creatures that crave interaction with others. Humans have the need to give and receive love; to feel like they belong in a group. When deprived of these needs, individuals may experience loneliness or depression.

Perfect family relationships and friendships are what an individual hope for. Not having a good family relationship, support from loved ones, and good friends, can make the individual feel lonely, which will not help him to satisfy his needs of love and belongingness.

To avoid problems such as loneliness, depression, and anxiety, it is important for us to have a healthy social life. Personal relationships with friends, family, and lovers play an important role, so as being associated with other groups like religious groups, sports teams, book clubs, etc. It falls into the category of "social belonging."

God has created us (humans) to long to belong, be loved, and to have the kind of companionship that can satisfy our inner-most emotional needs. That is what God meant when he said, "it is not good for man to be alone." **We want and need emotional companionship**. Without it, relationships in general, and marriage relationships more specifically, cannot enjoy the kind of intimacy God has designed for us to enjoy with the person we decide to marry.

There are a few things to keep in mind before we dive into some key emotional needs in a relationship. It is important to consider the following:

Emotional needs are not set in stone

You might have different needs throughout your life, and your needs can also shift within one relationship. This might happen as you learn more about yourself through personal growth or in relation to your partner and your development as a couple.

It is perfectly normal to adapt over time, even to discover needs you never considered before.

People can have different needs

Emotional needs vary from person to person. Some people might value belonging over love, or trust over desire, for example.

While you might prioritize certain things, such as attention and connectedness, your partner might place more importance on privacy and independence.

This does not mean your relationship is doomed, but you may need to put some extra effort into communicating needs and discussing ways to meet in the middle.

No one can meet all your needs

Emotional needs play an important part in relationship satisfaction. If they are fulfilled, you might feel contented, excited, or joyful. When they go unmet, on the other hand, you might feel frustrated, hurt, or confused.

That said, your partner *does not* have a responsibility to meet all your needs. Some needs, such as trust and communication, do affect relationship success. Without trust and openness, relationships typically do not work out long term.

But they cannot fulfill every need, and you should not expect them to.

The bottom line

As you may have noticed, getting needs met usually involves some collaborative problem-solving. And what does collaboration depend on? Good communication.

Discussing your needs with your partner is typically the best place to begin. If you cannot communicate, you probably cannot explore needs fulfillment together.

Struggling to get started? Couple's therapy can offer a safe, judgment-free space to begin talking through your concerns.

Your Partner Cannot Fulfill All Your Emotional Needs

You may feel that your spouse is not meeting your emotional needs. You should not consider yourself an empty emotional vessel to be filled by your spouse. You need to take responsibility for your own fulfillment, and the best way to do that is to consider and satisfy your spouse's needs first.

Meeting Your Spouse's Needs

An emotional need "is a craving that, when satisfied, leaves you with a feeling of happiness and contentment, and, when unsatisfied, leaves you with a feeling of unhappiness and frustration," says clinical psychologist and author, Dr. Willard F. Harley, Jr. https://www.verywellmind.com/the-purpose-of-emotions-2795181

His numerous books on marriage and relationships include *His Needs, Her Needs*, which focuses on the needs of men and women and shows husbands and wives how to satisfy those needs in their spouses. According to Harley, satisfying your own emotional needs means putting your spouse's desires ahead of your own.

TwoOfUs.org agrees, noting: "One of the keys to being successful in a long-term, committed relationship is properly understanding the emotional needs of your partner." You are not responsible for meeting *all* your partner's needs, the relationship website notes, but you certainly should put those needs ahead of your own. https://www.verywellmind.com/emotional-needs-not-filled-marriage-partner-2303305

Some of these needs include affection, conversation, honesty and openness, financial support, and family commitment. It is like the old saying: with love, the more you give, the more you get back.

65

Ask for What You Need

Once you are in the mindset of being a loving and giving spouse, you can then start to advocate for your own needs—but you must be careful about how you go about it.

When you want your spouse to perform some kind of action to magically meet your needs, you are really asking for them to change, says Barton Goldsmith, a psychotherapist and syndicated columnist for *Psychology Today*, and that's a nearly impossible request.

Instead, be direct. "Ask for what you need," says Goldsmith. "Do you want change, understanding, or compatibility? Whatever your need, asking for it directly will greatly improve your chances of getting it."

Show Your Spouse That You Care

It is at this point that the need for reciprocation comes into play. Continue to show your spouse that you value and care for them. Do those things that, generally, put your partner's needs ahead of your own.

"If someone feels valued, he or she will do the best they can to keep your opinion of them high," says Goldsmith. "Reminding your mate that you know your life is better because he or she is in it is very motivational and very loving."

Make sure you know what your partner wants and values: Is it a home-cooked meal? A spontaneous bouquet of flowers? A special dinner at a fancy restaurant or a quick burger at a fast-food eatery? Fixing that leaky faucet or loose door handle?

An Act of Kindness Goes a Long Way

It does not really matter what the act of kindness might be—the important thing is that your spouse knows they are valued—that you know what *they* want and need and that you are ready to provide it without being asked.

Take Responsibility for Yourself

Understand that you are in a relationship to bond with your spouse, to share events—big or small—and to build a life together.

"When we have an expectation that a husband or wife fulfill us, we set ourselves up for disappointment, because no human being can satisfy another human being," says Mark Altrogge, a pastor at an Indiana church, and creator of the relationship website the *Blazing Center*. "To hope that another human can meet our needs is asking too much of anyone."

"Don't look at where your spouse needs to change," Altrogge says. "Look to where you need to change. Do not have expectations of your spouse. If you have expectations, place them on yourself."

Robert Fulghum, in his classic book, "*All I Really Need to Know I Learned in Kindergarten*," explained it well in some of his basic rules: share everything, hold hands, and stick together.

If your partner knows that you care for them and will be there for them through big things and small, they are much more likely to reciprocate. Having your emotional needs met starts with sharing and caring for your partner. A person who feels loved, cared for, and appreciated is far more likely to reciprocate in kind.

10. Emotional Needs to Consider in Relationships

Everyone has emotional needs.

Consider basic survival needs like water, air, food, and shelter. Meeting these physical needs means you can stay alive, but it takes more to give life meaning.

You cannot see or touch things like companionship, affection, security, or appreciation, but they are just as valuable. The same goes for feeling heard or valued.

In a relationship, the strength of your bond can make a big difference in whether you both get your needs met.

Although every relationship looks a little different, these ten emotional needs are a good starting point for considering whether you and your partner are each getting what you need from the relationship.

1. Affection

Most relationships involve different kinds of affection:

- physical touch
- sexual intimacy
- loving words
- kind gestures

Affection helps you bond and increase closeness.

Not everyone shows affection in the same ways, but partners generally get used to each other's unique approaches toward fulfilling this need.

Someone who does not say "I love you" might show their regard through their actions, for example.

2. Acceptance

Knowing your partner accepts you as you are, can help create a sense of belonging in the relationship.

Acceptance does not just mean they accept *you*, though. It also means you feel as if you fit in with their loved ones and belong in their life.

This sense of belonging might increase when they:

- introduce you to family and friends
- plan activities to do together
- share dreams and goals for the future
- ask for advice when making decisions

If you do not feel accepted, you might feel as if you are hovering on the edges of their life. This is not a comfortable place to be.

Some people do not open up easily, and they might have other reasons for not including you in certain parts of their life. All the same, feeling like you do not belong can make it difficult for you to see yourself in the relationship long term.

Here is one strategy to try: If you have not already, invite them to meet *your* friends and family. Use this to open a conversation about how you would like to be more involved in their life.

3. Validation

Even the closest partners do not always see eye to eye, and that's okay. When you don't completely agree, though, you still want to know they've heard your concerns and understand where you're coming from.

According to research from 2016Trusted Source, most couples find it important to operate on the same wavelength. When your partner completely fails to see your perspective, you might feel misunderstood. If they dismiss your feelings entirely, you might feel ignored or disrespected.

If you generally feel validated, but this happens once or twice, it is possible they had an off day. It does not hurt to have a conversation, regardless, to share how you feel.

But if you consistently feel unheard or invalidated, you might start to build up some resentment, so it is best to address the issue sooner rather than later.

Try: "I haven't felt heard lately when I bring up important issues. Could we find a good time to have serious conversations, when we can both listen without distractions?"

4. Autonomy

As a relationship deepens, partners often begin sharing interests, activities, and other aspects of daily life. You might notice you are becoming more of a unit as you grow closer.

But no matter how strong your relationship becomes; it is essential to maintain your sense of self. While you might have plenty of things in common, you are two separate people with unique goals, hobbies, friends, and values–and that is a good thing.

If your identity has started to blur into theirs, take a step back to examine the situation. This blending of selves can happen naturally as you grow close, but it can also happen when you believe you need to become more like them for the relationship to succeed.

Maintaining individual interests can fuel curiosity about each other, which can strengthen your relationship and keep it fun. If you are losing sight of yourself before the relationship, set aside some time to reconnect with friends or restart an old hobby.

5. Security

A healthy relationship should feel secure, but security can mean many things.

If you feel secure in your relationship, you generally are:

- know they respect your boundaries
- feel safe to share your feelings
- feel physically safe with them
- believe they support your choices
- feel able to share your feelings

Setting clear boundaries can help boost your sense of security:

- "I don't want to be shouted at, so I won't respond if you raise your voice."

If your partner becomes abusive, seek professional support. Physical abuse is often easy to recognize, but emotional abuse can make you feel unsafe, too, even if you cannot put your finger on why.

6. Trust

Trust and security often go hand in hand. It is hard to feel physically or emotionally safe with someone you cannot trust. When you trust someone, you know they are looking out for you as well as themselves.

If you start to doubt them, try bringing up specific behaviors, such as staying out late without explanation. This helps you get to the bottom of what is going on while touching base on communication needs.

In general, trust does not happen immediately. You cultivate it over time, but you can also lose it in an instant. Broken trust can sometimes be repaired, but this requires effort from both partners and often, support from a therapist.

Be upfront about how you will handle breaches of trust in the relationship. While your specific response might vary based on the context of a given situation, you probably have a good idea about behaviors you cannot accept, such as infidelity or lying. Do not feel guilty about making those deal breakers known to your partner.

7. Empathy

Having empathy means you can imagine how someone else feels. This ability is essential to romantic relationships since it helps people understand each other and build deeper bonds.

Say they forget your birthday. You feel angry and hurt. After 5 years together, how could they? You have never forgotten *their* birthday.

But after your initial rush of disappointment and anger, you start to consider their side. They have been struggling at work lately, and that anxiety has started affecting their sleep. Most of their emotional energy has gone into planning a big project that could help turn things around.

With all that on their mind, you reason, it is more understandable how they completely blanked on your birthday. You know it was not an intentional slight, and you also know they feel terrible.

Your understanding of their situation helps you accept what happened and offer them compassion and forgiveness, which can bring you closer. Continuing to stew, on the other hand, might lead to an argument or drive you apart in other ways.

8. Prioritization

It is normal to want your partner to make you a priority. You want to know you come first and that after they meet their own needs, yours are next in line.

Of course, most people have a few (or more) significant relationships. From time to time, someone else in their life might need to come first, such as a friend going through a crisis or a family member experiencing a rough patch.

In general, though, if you do not feel like a priority in their life, you probably feel as if they don't really value your presence. This can make you wonder why they even bother with the relationship.

A conversation can often help. First, mention why you do not feel prioritized—try an I-statement to avoid sounding judgmental. Maybe they do not reply to your texts for a day or so, or consistently reschedule date night to catch up with friends.

Then suggest a possible solution, like replying to texts each evening or with a phone call or choosing a regular date night.

9. Connection

It is okay not to do *everything* together. In fact, maintaining separate interests and friendships can be good for individual emotional health, as well as the health of your relationship (see autonomy above).

But you probably want to feel connected at the same time. That is perfectly understandable. What are relationships for, if not sharing your life?

Without connection, you can feel lonely even when you spend most of your time together. It might seem as if you are just two people who happen to share a living space or spend time together sometimes. Chances are good that is not how you want your relationship to proceed.

Here is the good news: If you lack this sense of connection, it's completely possible to reconnect and engage with them again.

Some helpful tips:

- Ask questions about an aspect of their daily life you have never really thought about before.
- Suggest a new activity to try together.
- Break out of your usual routine by taking a day or weekend trip.
- Bond over shared memories or swap individual ones from your childhood.

10. Space

Connection is important, but so is space.

Space within a relationship means you both have the freedom to do your own thing when you want to. You feel supported but know you can make your own choices.

It also means you still enjoy some privacy. This privacy can mean separate spaces to work or relax at home, but it also means emotional privacy.

Being honest does not mean you need to share every thought that crosses your mind. If you feel annoyed, for example, getting some physical and emotional space can help you work through these thoughts in healthy ways and avoid taking things out on your partner.

When it comes to space, asking for what you need is key.

Consider: carving out a bit of alone time each day; creating a private space for yourself at home, whether that's a separate room or a little nook; or spending more time outside.

Being "alone" has little to do with how many people are around you. Or how busy or active your life is.

Not being alone, as God identified it for Adam, has more to do with *who* is around you. It has to do with the fulfilled relational need one gets to enjoy when the right companion understands you and loves you enough (or even loves you SO much) that they look for ways to satisfy that deep need inside of you. We are then emotionally filled every day.

What a magnificent blessing to love and be loved like that! God knew what Adam needed. He knows what we need as well.

A Side Note:

We are made in the likeness of God to be capable of giving and receiving love through emotional fulfillment. God receives our love *to* Him when we live our lives in obedience to Him. Yes, He can "feel" that love because it is a spiritual exchange of emotion. We, too, can receive love *from* God, through His Spirit that we receive in us when we invite Him into our hearts.

Do not miss out on His love!

In summary-the significance of companionship:

To finish up this learned Lesson #3 - It is Not Good to Be Alone - *Man's Deepest Need Identified*, let us summarize what we have discussed:

1. God recognized a need that Adam had as he obediently went about the work God had given him to do ("it's not good for man to be alone").

2. Regardless of the number of creatures in Adam's path, none could fulfill the need that Adam had; only someone uniquely made for you can do that.

3. God sees what we need long before we do. And He sets things in motion for our needs to be met. Because that is what love does!

4. Humans were created with an innate need for companionship. The need for closeness, friendship, belonging, and love.

5. Our emotional need for belonging must be met for us to enjoy intimate relationship with our spouses and others.

6. At times you may feel that your spouse is not meeting your emotional needs. You need to take responsibility for your own fulfillment, and the best way to do that is to consider and satisfy your spouse's needs first.

7. We are made in the likeness of God to be capable of giving and receiving love. God receives our love *to* Him when we live our lives in submission to Him. We receive love *from* God, through His Spirit that we receive in us when we invite Him into our hearts.

CHAPTER 6

Lesson 4: There is a Unique Solution for Man's Deepest Need – *A Suitable Helper (Genesis 2:18-22a)*

18 *The Lord God said, "It is not good for the man to be alone. I will make <u>a helper suitable for him</u>."*

19 *Now the Lord God had formed out of the ground all the wild animals and all the birds in the sky. He brought them to the man to see what he would name them; and whatever the man called each living creature, that was its name.* **20** *So the man gave names to all the livestock, the birds in the sky and all the wild animals.*

But for Adam no suitable helper was found. **21** *So the Lord God caused the man to fall into a deep sleep; and while he was sleeping, he took one of the man's ribs and then closed up the place with flesh.* **22** *Then the Lord God made a woman from the rib he had taken out of the man.*

"It is not good for the man to be alone." As we detailed in learned Lesson #3 – God recognized a void in Adam that needed to be filled. That need was for companionship. All the other creatures had a mate ("after their kind"), but not Adam.

Consequently, God said, "I will make a helper suitable for him." (Genesis 2:18).

Even as Adam went about naming all the creatures there was no creature capable of providing the emotional fulfillment that would satisfy that need.

After this long and unsatisfying experience as a lonely bachelor, God saw that Adam was emotionally prepared for a companion—a "suitable helper." Adam was now emotionally prepared for a wife!

God then subjected Adam to a deep sleep, removed from his body the bone that was closest to his heart, and from that physical core of man fashioned the first woman.

Man and Woman were created in the image and likeness of God. Most of the uses of the word "image" (or "representation") in the Old Testament are to designate an idol shaped in the form of a person or an animal. "Likeness" is a word of comparison. It is used to attempt to explain something referring to something else that it is like.

Although God makes it clear that there is no way we can understand him by comparing him to a person or thing (Isaiah 40:18), we can understand the nature of man by comparing human beings with the Lord (Genesis 1:26).

The creation story makes it clear that the likeness - image is not of physical form: material for creation was taken from the earth. ***It is the inner nature of human beings that reflects something vital in God.***

Thus, theologians generally agree that the likeness is rooted in all that is required to make a human being a person: in our intellectual, emotional, and moral likeness to God, who has revealed himself to us as a personal being. (The Encyclopedia of Bible Words; 1985, 1991).

Mankind (male and female) is distinguished from all other creatures in two respects: he alone is made in God's own likeness; and he is given charge over all the rest of creation.

But who is this newly formed creation? What is so unique about her? Why is she like Adam, yet not like Adam? And what makes her such a "suitable helper" anyway?

In this learned Lesson #4, we will attempt to answer each of these queries.

Let us see if we can get a grasp of who this creature is, and why she was so important in providing companionship for Adam, and instrumental in his emotional fulfillment.

Who is she?

The woman, who is she? Good question. First, she is a female human being. She is a new being yet sharing the man's own essential nature.

They both had the same nature. But what man lacked (his aloneness was not good) she supplied, and what she lacked he supplied.

The first step to cure Adam's aloneness was the creation of the woman to be his partner – the fitting into a unity in which each helps the other equally.

Formed from Adam's rib, or side – symbolizes their shared identity as together sharing dominion over the earth (Genesis

1:27,28), as expressed in Adam's exclamation that the woman was "bone of my bones and flesh of my flesh" (Genesis 2:23).

Symbolic of the unity of marriage, God made the woman bone of his bones, and flesh of his flesh. Together, the pair were to live in the beautiful garden, which was adapted to their needs and happiness. A relationship of holy fellowship between Creator and creature was to be maintained by simple obedience.

Here was the beginning of the first family, which God blessed and joined together to multiply or increase upon the earth.

This is the kind of "suitable helper" God had in mind. Better said, she was a "helper" who was created to be "suitable" for him.

A Helper for him

Traditionally, the English word "helper" can connote so many different ideas, which does not accurately convey the connotation of the Hebrew word. Usage of the Hebrew term does not suggest a subordinate role, a connotation which English "helper" can have.

In the Bible God is frequently described as the "helper," the one who does for us that we cannot do for ourselves, the one who meets our needs. In this context the word seems to express the idea of an "indispensable companion." The woman would supply what the man was lacking in the design of creation and logically it would follow that the man would supply what she was lacking.

Eve's identification as a "helper suitable for him" (Genesis 2:18,20) does not imply subordination or inferiority, but identity. Only a being with the same personal capacities and capabilities as Adam could have related to him. God himself is called the believer's helper (Psalm 33:20; Psalm 46:1).

Because of the "suitable" nature of her design, she intuitively knows her husband's needs because of the intimacy of their relationship.

A Side Note:

Two great and distinctly different quotes capture the role of this new creature Adam called, Woman.

> *"Often we can help each other most by leaving each other alone; at other times we need the hand-grasp and the word of cheer"*
>
> [Elbert Hubbard – *The Notebook*]
>
> *"She holds up an ideal of a higher type – a woman who shall be man's Intellectual companion, and his helper in the battle of life"*
>
> [L. Higgin and Eugene E. Street – *Spanish Life in Town and Country*]

The Lord God said, *"I will make a helper suitable for him."*

But what is meant by the term "helper"?

Definition: Helper – a person who helps another person or group with a job they are doing; a person who gives assistance, support, etc.

To fully grasp the magnitude of the role of the woman God created for Adam, it is good to look at several synonyms for the word *helper*: companion, partner, ally, supporter, mate, collaborator, right-hand person, helpmate, backer, friend, colleague, "main man" (or woman).

God's perfect design of the woman as "helper" was (and is) a role no other creature could adequately and completely fulfill for man.

The literal Hebrew translation might be "a help as one standing opposite him," or "a help as his counterpart."

What does she "help" him do?

The helper that God created the woman to be is one who "comes alongside him" to help her husband accomplish his purpose as the leader. She was a companion for him—a counterpart.

As said above, in the Bible God is frequently described as the "helper," the one who does for us that we cannot do for ourselves, the one who meets our needs. In this context the word seems to express the idea of an "indispensable companion."

It was not good for the man to be alone doing what God had purposed him to do. In view of that, He created a creature much like Adam who intuitively understood what Adam needed to accomplish his purposes. In that, she would become that "indispensable companion" united with

Adam to accomplish what is now *their* purpose.

What was she to help Adam do? Let us look back at the responsibilities God gave him.

1. Work the Garden (Gen. 2:15)

2. Maintain the Garden (Gen. 2:15)

3. Name the animals and creatures (Gen. 2: 19,20)

4. Be fruitful and multiply (Gen. 1:28)

5. Fill the earth and subdue it (Gen. 1:28)

6. Provide leadership and authority over fish, birds, and every living thing that moves on the earth (Gen. 1:28).

The interesting thing is the first three directives were given specifically to Adam. The last three were given to both. There is shared responsibility, shared accountability, and shared consequences for non-compliance. This "helper" is not one who is expected to just "do what you are told." Oh no, this is an equal partnership with equal accountability, although the roles are separately defined (man/woman).

A Side Note:

In relationships, it is imperative that a man knows his purpose and is doing that which is fulfilling and value-added, before saying "I do" to this intuitively supportive partner. What is she to help you do (man) if you are not actively pursuing "work"? Just know, she is designed by nature (like man) to take responsibility to get things done. If you do not want her to step into the leadership role in the relationship, be the responsible leader, and lead your family well by working hard at that which is your God-given pursuit.

Not only was this woman created to help the man accomplish his purpose, she also intuitively understood what help he needed, and how to help him.

Additionally, **she was created to provide the type of companionship that no other creature could provide.** She was "suitable" for him.

Suitable for him

The Lord God said, *"I will make a helper <u>suitable</u> for him."*

But what is meant by the term "suitable"?

Definition: <u>Suitable</u> – an adjective that means right for a particular person, purpose, or situation

Synonyms for suitable: appropriate; acceptable; able; qualified; compatible; complementary befitting; fit; suited; cut out for; right; reasonable; proper

The woman was a perfectly suited partner. She was comparable to Adam and was the appropriate creature to meet man's most intimate and emotional needs.

A suitable wife is compatible with her husband in many respects– physically, mentally, emotionally, and spiritually. This does not mean the man and woman are the same in everything, only that they fit together in harmony. They complement each other.

The B-flat key on the piano is not the same as the G, but together they make a harmonious chord. Similarly, *a suitable helper for a husband is a wife who is different from him, but well-suited to him, one who completes him in every way and who brings harmony, not discord, to the relationship.*

Wives are to be as the picture of the church submitting to Christ, and husbands are to be like Jesus in giving himself up for her (his wife) like Jesus did. That is the ideal picture of why God used Adam's rib to make the woman (later called Eve), each significantly completing the other. Not that each one was not complete in himself or herself with unique and varied gifts and talents, but that each was made to be the crown of the other, equal and a fitting companion.

The Hebrew word translated "fit" is *kenegdow*. It literally means "according to the opposite of him." In other words, the focus is on an appropriate match. Eve was not created above or below Adam; she was complementary. The animals Adam had named each had an appropriate companion (Genesis 2:20), and Adam was now given a fitting companion as well. Eve was "just right" for him.

Further, God's statement that it was not good for man to be alone implies that Adam was lonely and incomplete by himself. He had been created for relationship, and it is impossible to have relationship alone. With the creation of Eve, Adam experienced the joy of love for another person.

A man is, by nature, a social creature; God created us to need companionship. And, of course, a man alone cannot propagate. Adam by himself was incomplete. Therefore, God created Eve as a "helper fit for him", to complete Adam, to provide society for him, and to enable him to produce children.

Eve was exactly what Adam needed—a helper suitable for him.

She was equal to him, opposite of him, able to help, a companion, one who would speak up and advise, and face the joys and sorrows of life together. They would complete each other. Each one had a mind to think, a heart to feel, and a spirit that would live forever.

A Side Note:

As you will read in the "About the Authors" section of this book, it mentions the request made to God to "present to me the woman He had prepared to be my 'suitable helper'." Well, God certainly answered that request with the most perfect "fit" for me. Carol is uniquely different from me, but inside our hearts (where it really counts), she is very much like me.

Our values, life goals, love for God, our generosity, love for people, and our commitment to serve others in obedience to God and His purpose for us together, are all a "perfect fit."

Additionally, her ability to love me the way I need to be loved, and her keen understanding of what I need, and how to meet those specific needs, continues to amaze me and affords me an even greater love for her every day.

This is how God designed the woman to be as the perfect companion for man.

In view of that, does this mean that every man must have a wife, a helper to complete him? No. In fact, the apostle Paul said that celibacy is a good thing for the servant of God (1 Cor. 7:7-9). Does it mean that every woman must be a wife and a completer of a man? No. Not every woman wants to marry or is led to matrimony.

However, the Genesis passage sets the standard for most people in most contexts. A wife is the helper suitable for her husband.

In summary-the significance of a suitable helper:

To finish up this learned Lesson #4 – There is a Unique Solution for Man's Deepest Need – *A Suitable Helper*, let us summarize what we have discussed:

1. God recognized that, unlike the other creatures, Adam had no helper (which he needed) that was suitable (a companion) for him.

2. So God fashioned a woman from Adam's rib. She was a female human being. She was a new being yet sharing the man's own essential nature.

3. What the man lacked she supplied, and what she lacked he supplied.

4. This *helper* that God created the woman to be, was one who "comes alongside him" to help her husband accomplish his purpose as the leader. She was a companion for him.

5. The woman was a perfectly suited partner. She was comparable to Adam and was the appropriate creature to meet man's most intimate and emotional needs.

6. Adam was lonely and incomplete by himself. *He had been created for relationship*, and it is impossible to have relationship alone. With the creation of Eve, Adam experienced the joy of love for another person.

7. A suitable helper for a husband is a wife who is different from him, but well-suited to him, who completes him in every way, and who brings harmony, not discord, to the relationship.

CHAPTER 7

Lesson 5: Your Woman is a Gift – *A Very Special Delivery (Genesis 2:22b)*

"Then the Lord God made a woman from the rib he had taken out of the man, <u>and he brought her to the man.</u>"

G od subjected Adam to a deep sleep, removed from his body the bone that was closest to his heart, and from that physical core of man fashioned the first woman. Although God *created* man from the dust of the earth, he took his time and *fashioned* this first woman. This one was incredibly special, and specially made.

He *brought* her to the man! God did not just tell her to *go to the man*; He delivered her to the man himself. God presented the woman to Adam in all her fresh, unspoiled beauty, and Adam was ecstatic with joy! (More on that in learned Lesson #6).

Women who place their hands in God's hand can trust him to place them in the hands of the right men.

(Carol) Placing my hands in the hands of God came with a strong desire to finally find the right man after past failures trying to do it on my own. I made the conscious decision to stay in prayer and allow God to lead me to the man He has selected for me. By walking in faith and continued trust in God's guidance, I knew one day He would bring the right and perfect husband for me. One who could love me in the same way that God designed Adam to love Eve. Although I knew with God all things are possible, I NEVER thought the one for me would be someone like Terry! (Because we are so different!). Yet, God knew what and who was best for me. My life is now complete and there is pure joy in my heart because of God's choice for me. It was the best decision ever!

God delivering (or presenting) the woman to the man, signifies just how special she was to him. With time and great care was she fashioned, from a significant part of the man, for the purpose of being given back to the man.

Today, in most marriage ceremonies, there is a caring person (usually the father) who is asked "who gives this bride away?" The act of "presenting" the bride to the groom is symbolic of the same act God demonstrated in this first "marriage." The bride (woman) is someone incredibly special to the father (God) and great trust for her continued love and care is now being placed into the hands of another man. This is what makes this delivery so special!

Another significant part of this first "marriage ceremony" was not only the act of the giver, but the gift itself (the woman).

What is a gift?

Definition: Something *given* voluntarily without payment in return, as to show favor toward someone, or to honor an occasion; a present.

Gifts are so much a part of so many occasions. But choosing them, buying them, wrapping them, and presenting them are an indispensable part of the excitement and joy.

We give gifts to people we know. We give special gifts to those we love. Often, we try to make the gift special. Somebody in the family loves novels, so we look for a bestseller in fiction. Someone else works outdoors, so we shop for a pair of warm gloves.

Gift giving is something that should not be a chore. It must come from the heart. When you give gifts, you are giving something willingly without wanting something in return. Making someone feel special is more than enough reason to make you give more. It tells the receiver that you were thinking about them.

While it feels good to be on the receiving end, there is a feeling of self-gratification when you are the one who is doing the giving. (See Acts 20:35 where Paul referenced words that Jesus himself said: *"We are more happy when we give than when we receive."*) (New Life Version).

This cannot be measured by monetary value. The happiness you get from opening a gift is only temporary but giving provides a more self-fulfilling experience that lasts for a long period of time.

No matter what the reason is for giving a gift, **the best presents are those that come from the heart.**

The Packaging Makes a Difference

After acquiring the gift, we wrap it in bright, colorful paper, tied not with string, but with gleaming ribbon. Why? It is special. Why? The recipient is special to us. According to Wikipedia, in many cultures, gifts are traditionally packaged in some way. For example, in Western cultures, gifts are often wrapped in wrapping paper and accompanied by a gift note which may note the occasion, the recipient's name and the giver's name.

A great deal of time, effort, and thought goes into the acquiring (or making) of a gift. Then great time and attention goes into properly packaging (or wrapping) the gift, and then delivering of that special gift to that special someone.

Every gift is unique. Yet, what all gifts have in common is, it's a *gift*! It is something specially prepared, and specifically intended, for that one special person. Both the gift and the recipient are special to the giver.

Obviously, the man (Adam) was special to God. He was God's very first human creation on earth. Thus, it stands to reason He wanted to create a special gift to be given to this special man.

But what is so special about THIS gift?

Good question.

There are many aspects of this gift that makes her so special. We will discuss a few:

First, she was specially made for the man. Don't you just love getting gifts that you can really use, versus that big ugly tie, or that hard fruit cake you used to get for Christmas? Useful gifts that are purchased or made because it is something YOU want, generally are more gratifying than ones given because it was something the *giver* wanted you to have.

Don't get me wrong, you still accept the gift, but the gratification at the heart level may be missing. You must admit, getting that 75-inch, latest model, flat-screen TV for your "man cave" scores greater points on the receiving scale than an equally as thoughtful abstract painting of obscure landscapes!

This gift that God gave to Adam was something he *really* needed. What Adam needed was companionship, from another human being; a puppy (although cute) would not do! God created this woman specifically in a way that would satisfy that need, packaged her so attractively and deliberately, and then presented her to Adam.

Second, she was uniquely made. She was different from all the other creatures that Adam ever saw up to this time. The woman had unique characteristics and traits that made her the perfect gift to meet Adam's specific needs:

1. She had human-like features like him, but she was a softer, gentler, more attractive version. Adam recognized the similarities when he named her "woman", which loosely translates as "like man." But God knew how important it was for this gift to be attractive to Adam if there was ever going to be "baby Adams" and "little Eves" running around! After all, He did command them to be fruitful and multiply!

2. She was intellectually compatible so she could adapt to her new surroundings in the Garden and help Adam with the purposes and responsibilities given to them. Additionally, given her intellectual compatibility, they must have had great conversations about animal names!

3. She was equally as industrious and did not mind doing her part to keep the Garden beautiful. Can you imagine what it would have been like if God had made the woman unwilling to help do the work? Conflict! Of course, we know that would not have been the case because God is way too wise for that

to have happened, and she was created with the "helper gene" because that was her created nature to begin with. His goal was to make a "helper" suitable for him.

4. She had the ability to relate to Adam on an emotional level. For once Adam had someone with whom he could express love and affection. The companionship he longed for as a created human being had been missing for oh so long! Now this beautiful gift given to him was just what was needed. She could fully relate to him, and him to her, she provided something that he never experienced before. One writer put it so eloquently like this:

"A beautiful woman, her love just fits with you. She shares your deepest personal views and understands you. When you talk to her, you feel like she is miles ahead of you, yet at the same time she makes you feel perfect and beautiful as well. Because of whom she is inside, it rubs off on who she is outside. She simply glows. Every slight imperfection becomes a perfection, and just completes her." – ThisIsTruth. (https://www.urbandictionary.com/author.php?author=ThisIsTruth)

What a beautiful gift for every man to have!

Third, she came with no instructions. The third aspect of this gift that made it so special is that she came with no instructions - none were needed (for now). Most gifts, especially the more complicated ones, usually come with instructions. Why didn't this one? A few reasons:

1. No "assembly" was required. She came perfectly packaged, perfectly assembled, and perfectly presented. No assembly instructions were required because she was already well-put-together! Fully assembled and ready for "use!"

2. She was created with the intuitive nature to do what her purpose was to do, meet her husband's needs. She was fully prepared to come alongside to help Adam in whatever capacity required. She knew her purpose and was fully content fulfilling it. That is what happens when all parts are fully functioning as the creator designed them to. Things work smoothly, no extra effort or instructions required.

3. This relationship was truly a "match made in heaven." There was no need for an instructional manual on "how to relate to your spouse" or, "improving your communication style", or "how to love your spouse." They were emotionally compatible and intuitively knew how to meet each other's emotional needs. Their relationship just worked the way the designer intended it to work, effortlessly and automatically, with trust, honesty, respect, and unwavering love.

A Side Note:

It was purposedly stated above that the woman came with no instructions because none were needed - *for now*. This is a salient side note for a couple reasons; (1) it would be unrealistic to think all marriage relationships today have the same emotional compatibility as the "first couple" did in the beginning. But that is both the problem and the solution. The problem is that in many relationships today, couples do not experience the love and connection that comes when lovingly meeting each other's emotional needs, as was experienced in the Garden. The solution then, conceptually, is quite simple....do what they did! But alas, therein lies the rub, which leads to the second problem; (2) **we are unable to do what they did** (have a oneness relationship experienced through genuine self-sacrificing love), **because we do not have what they had** (a heart of pure love created in them by the Designer), **until we get back to**

being who they were (unblemished created beings made in the image of the Creator, who *is* love)!

See, here is the problem: in Genesis 3:15, after Adam and Eve's sin and the resulting consequences imputed by God, to Adam he said, "I will put *enmity* between you and the woman." Oh my! There it is! That is why there were no instructions required for this gift - until now. Because now, because of THEIR disobedience to God, mankind's once intuitive, beautifully fulfilling, and loving relationship with their spouse has become one of conflict, hostility, and contentiousness. That is just what sin will do. Subsequently, now for us, to get back to the kind of relationship that was easy before the Fall, we now must get back to being who God made us to be. For that, we need instructions on how to love like God intends us to love, and how to unselfishly give ourselves to each other as they did.

That requires a renewing of our mind and hearts through the love and grace provided in our relationship with Christ Jesus. He can renew us and restore us so that we can once again enjoy the kind of fulfilling emotional relationship and compatibility our first parents enjoyed in the beginning.

May God deliver to every man and every woman, that "special delivery" of the kind of "gift" that is just what you needed and always wanted!

In summary-the significance of this special delivery:

To finish up this learned Lesson #5 - Your Woman is a Gift-*A Very Special Delivery*, let us summarize what we have discussed:

1. Although God *created* man from the dust of the earth, he took his time and *fashioned* the first woman.

2. He *brought* her to the man! God did not just tell her to *go to the man*. He delivered her to the man himself. God presented the woman to Adam in all her fresh, unspoiled beauty.

3. We give gifts to people we know. We give special gifts to those we love. Why? Because it demonstrates how special the gift and the recipient are to us. So, it was with God's gift to Adam.

4. Every gift is unique. It is specially prepared, and specifically intended for that one special person. The woman was specifically fashioned by God, as a needed gift to Man.

5. The woman was specially made for the man. This gift that God gave to Adam was something he really needed. Adam needed companionship, from another human being. Not only was this a gift he *needed*, but it was also one he really *wanted*!

6. The woman was uniquely made. She was different from all the other creatures. Her most unique quality was she had the ability to relate to Adam on an emotional level. Which gave them the ability to love and be loved. We all need that!

7. The woman required no instructions (until later). She came perfectly packaged, perfectly assembled, and perfectly presented! No "assembly" was required.

CHAPTER 8

Lesson 6: The First Response Says It All– *Your Appreciation Shows (Genesis 2:23)*

"At last! A suitable companion, a perfect partner! Bone from my bones. Flesh from my flesh. I will call this one 'woman' as an eternal reminder that she was taken out of man."

What do you do with a gift? No, not just any gift–THAT gift! You know the one. Yes, that one. The one that you want SO badly that almost every day you *remind* someone of how much you want that gift! If the gift you so desperately want is in a store, every time you are in that store, you must show that desired gift to the person(s) being dragged along just so they can see the gift... again!

If the gift you long for is online, you take screenshots of the expectant gift, continue to show the picture to your loved one, and even forward it to their inbox multiple times, just for that subtle "hint, hint", to fully establish with them the vision of your expectation.

Then, after so many days, or months, or perhaps even years, it finally happens! Yes, that gift you have been longing for, dreaming of, waiting patiently (okay maybe not so patiently) for so awfully long, Now, there it is! You FINALLY have that incredibly beautiful, gloriously special, amazingly spectacular gift, for which you have waited for so long!

Now what? What do you DO with this kind of gift?

In the previous chapter, learned lesson #5 described the incredibly special gift God prepared for Adam. It was a unique gift specially made for Adam. Once this hand crafted, beautifully fashioned gift was finally prepared, God then made a special delivery of this special gift when he *brought her to the man.*" (Genesis 2:22).

He *brought* her to the man! God did not just tell her to *go to the man*; He delivered her to the man himself. And Adam was ecstatic with joy!

Genesis 2 closes with a vivid portrayal of Adam's joyous acceptance of his new helpmate and his unreserved commitment to her in love.

Gifts are special and they are unique. And once a gift is given, the expectation is the gift will be appreciated due to all the time, care, and thoughtfulness given to it.

In view of that, what was Adam's response to this gift he needed and wanted for so long? Adam's first response was this: *"At last! a suitable companion, a perfect partner! Bone from my bones. Flesh from my flesh. I will call this one 'woman' as an eternal reminder that she was taken out of man!"*

The first response says it all.

Can you sense the elation in Adam's response? Can you tell how excited he is to, finally, get that special gift he so desperately wanted?

Adam's response reflects two principles that are relevant to relationships.

The first is, the **"principle of first response"**. This principle, usually related to conflict in relationships, suggests that your initial reaction to an incident may escalate the situation. But if you stop and think first, your initial response to the incident can calm the situation.

Although the reference here is not regarding conflict (far from it), there is applicability of this principle when you look at the power of a first response. In this case Adam's elated response to the special gift, he received was so impromptu, so unrehearsed, and so genuine, that it had to make the gift-giver (God) pleased, as well as the gift (the woman) feel exceptionally appreciated and warmly embraced.

The principle of the first response is predicated on how one feels about the situation, or in this case how Adam felt about his gift, the woman. It is obvious that he was ecstatic and therefore those involved in the exchange also walked away feeling good.

The first response can escalate an already bad moment. But a positive first response can bring calm, pleasantness, and the feeling of grateful appreciation. This then elevates the intimacy in a relationship in an incredibly positive manner.

The second principle identified by Adam's response is the **"principle of first impression."**

It is said that your first impression is a lasting one.

As defined by *Wikipedia*: in psychology, a first impression is the event when one person first encounters another person and forms a mental image of that person. The first impressions individuals give to others could greatly influence how they are treated and viewed in many contexts of everyday life.

It takes just one-tenth of a second for us to judge someone and make a first impression. Research finds that the more time participants are afforded to form the impression, the more confidence in impressions they report. Not only are people quick to form first impressions, but they are also fairly accurate when the target presents him or herself genuinely.

An online article in *Psychology Today* states: "Human beings are built to size each other up quickly. These first impressions are influenced by a number of factors, such as facial shape, vocal inflection, attractiveness, and general emotional state. People tend to get attached to their initial impressions of others and find it difficult to change their opinion, even when presented with lots of evidence to the contrary."

Whereas the "principle of first response" is predicated on *how you feel* about something; the "principle of first impression" is predicated on what *you see when you see something* or someone.

As noted above, how you first see someone will impact how you treat them. Imagine how Adam's gift (the woman) is going to be treated based on Adam's first impression of her? This is the significant lesson to take from this chapter. As a matter of fact, this is probably THE lesson of the entire book!

How a man treats his wife, and a wife treats her husband, will largely hinge on how they see each other. How he sees her is largely impacted by his first impressions of her, the same her with him. If no further evidence to the contrary, we will rely on and react based on our first impressions. First impressions are lasting impressions.

Here is one other connected and interesting take away from Adam's reaction when receiving his gift. It is in what he *called* her.

When Adam first saw the Woman (his gift) remember what he said? He said, *"I will call this one 'woman' as an eternal reminder that she was taken out of man."*

Remember one of the major assignments God gave Adam in the Garden? It was to name all the animals, birds, and other creatures. This was no small task. There were hundreds of creatures to name. Each one came to Adam and what he called it, that was its name.

Adam gained expertise from that experience enabling him to accurately decide what to name the creature based on what he saw. That insight imparted in him the knowledge to accurately "name" this new gift given to him.

The name he gave to the woman reflected the appreciation for his gift even more.

Two points:

1. Adam *called* her what he *saw* her to be: Woman - "like a man"- similar but different.

She was unique and uniquely different from all the other creatures. **Adam saw her uniqueness.** To fully appreciate anything, you must accurately see it for what it is. If you jump into a rowboat and expect to speed out to sea, you are going to be extremely disappointed. You must see it for what it is.

The same with those you are in relationship with. You must see them for who they are. In Proverbs 18:22 it says, *"The man who finds a wife finds a treasure. To choose an adulteress is both stupid and ungodly."*

The application here is in seeing the person as they really are. Finding a *wife* is a treasure. But if the one you choose before marriage is not "wife material" – it is unrealistic to think she will behave like one.

Same goes for the woman choosing a man to marry. You want an industrious, hard-working provider who loves and adores you for who you are. But if you get serious about a guy who is "tall, dark, and handsome", but still "looking" for a job at 40 years old, and still lives at home with his mother with his babies' mamas (plural); you realistically cannot expect him to be that mature "husband-man" you want him to be.

Properly identifying what you see (in a person) helps you make good choices and decisions before marriage. When a man makes that right choice to marry, he probably thinks of her and calls her things like "my gift", or "the one I always dreamed of." If so, then during the life of your marriage continue seeing her uniqueness and continue calling her things like, "my treasure", "my gift", "my angel", "uniquely mine", "my love", "my precious queen." You get the point. What you call her, is what she will be. *You have the power in your tongue!*

Women see the greatness in your man. Yes, that same man whom you adored before marriage because you proudly saw him as "the man", or "my man!" After getting married, continue calling him things like, "my man"; "my superman"; "my hand-some man"; my loving man"; "my gentle-man"; or "my super-hero!" *Your words will empower him and cause him to want to live up to what you see him to be.*

What you call your spouse is what they will be.

2. Adam *called* her who he *understood* her to be. From him – part of him – connected to him.

Adam knew that the woman was part of him. Upon receipt of this gift, he exclaimed that she was *"bone of my bones and flesh of my flesh."* Adam knew where this gift came from.

Two points:

1. Adam knew this woman (gift) came **from him**. He knew she was part of him because she was taken from him. This woman looked like him, the very image of himself – but different. Being "like him" was great cause to love her, like he loved himself! (see Jesus' words to all mankind in Mark 12:31 – "love your neighbor as yourself.").

Loving your spouse should be a natural outcome from understanding that you are part of one another.

Love who you are then you will love who is part of you!

2. Adam knew this woman (gift) came **from God**. When it is understood that your gift came from someone special, it adds a greater significance to the gift. When you fully understand and appreciate the fact that your "gift" (spouse) comes from God, who "brought" your gift to you, changes how you treat your gift. When you appreciate that this gift is "God's handiwork", you should value the gift even more. Then you will understand that this gift (spouse) should be treated extra special!

(Carol) Because Terry understands that a wife is a gift given by God, he treats me in a manner pleasing to God. He calls me his "answered prayer", and his "gift from God." I truly feel like I am a gift based on Terry's prayer, *"present to me the woman you have prepared to be my suitable helper."* This is the same way God prepared Eve when He fashioned (or prepared) her for Adam. By God preparing me to be a helper suitable for Terry, he recognized the gift that God prepared for him and received me as his gift. I feel the love and appreciation Terry shows me as his gift. He cherishes me. This makes me want to love him more, and in turn, make him feel that he is special too.

What you call your spouse is what they will be.

If your impression (what you see) is not accurate, then your response (what you do) will be detrimental to the relationship. You will call it what it is not. There is power in your tongue! Negative, hurtful, or demeaning words spoken to your spouse, that attack their character and nature, will damage the oneness desired in the relationship. Watch what you say!

On the other hand, when you accurately see your gift (your spouse) as a uniquely created, awesomely magnificent, adoringly special companion perfectly suited for you, your response will be more like Adam's: Wow! A woman at last! She is beautiful! I have never seen anything like her! Man, this is what I have been looking for!

The woman may look at her special gift of a man and exclaim; OMG, do you see this man! He is off the chain gorgeous! Look at that physique! I love those eyes! I can see that he is so loving and caring! He will treat me like a queen! He is the man of my dreams! He is all I have ever wanted and needed!

Just think what would happen if all men and women entered the marriage relationship with that type of excitement, enthusiasm, and joy for one another. An excitement and elation based on an accurate understanding of who that future mate is and how uniquely fitting they are to all you ever wanted and needed.

When each person is intrinsically ecstatic due to that deep-inside-the-soul feeling, knowing that **THIS IS THE ONE** God has specially created and specifically fashioned to be your soul-connected companion, who fulfills you deep within the very depths of your being…*would you ever want to leave a person like that?* Why would you? There would be *a forever commitment to love and care for your gift until death you did part.*

That is doing relationship like God intended!

A Side Note:

It was stated above that this chapter probably presents **the** most important lesson in this book.

Here is what is meant by that.

Over the years of working with married couples, and from the authors' own previous marriage, it is apparent that we have missed the significance of the power of the first impression and the first response. Most marriages do not begin with the thrill and excitement Adam showed when God presented his gift (the woman) to him.

Not that most marriages do not begin with excitement. For sure they do. But the excitement for most tends to be the excitement of *getting* married, the excitement of the ceremony or the honeymoon. Some are excited about having sex or sharing a residence for financial ease.

Yet, the thrill that comes from truly knowing who this person is, where this person came from, and the understanding of the specialness of the one who gave the gift to you, is sorely lacking. As a result, we rarely learn to recognize the significant value of the "gift", or how to fully appreciate the "gift" or the "gift-giver."

What we don't appreciate, we don't value. What we don't value we don't maintain. What we don't maintain it deteriorates. This has been the demise of many marriages and other significant relationships.

What a wonderful thing it would be if marriages today started like this "first marriage" - with excitement, and pure joy, not just about the wedding day, but with an elated heart of genuine love and appreciation for one another. Additionally, there would be a commitment to honor, respect, and cherish one another with adoration for the one who gave you just what you wanted. This commitment compels you to give the rest of your life to the one who gives the best of life! (Both God and your suitable companion whom you call "my loving partner for life!").

If marriages today started like this "first marriage"–then love wouldn't fade; commitment wouldn't wane, and the "disrupter" of all things good (Satan) would not win by destroying the beauty of the marriage relationship. What God has joined together, let no one separate (Matthew 19:6).

That is why this chapter is key in having successful marriages and preventing divorce. If every marriage started like, and remained like, the "first marriage", perhaps, then, divorce would no longer be an issue.

Because, in the beginning it (divorce) was not so.

Let us start all marriage relationships with the joy of Adam, the heart of God, and the appreciation for the blessing in receiving such a great and special gift from our Father!

What do you do with THIS special Gift?

Now you finally have the gift you always wanted. You are excited and appreciative of this special gift. But what do you *do* with *this* gift (this woman; this man)?

Here are a few ideas to help answer that question:

1. You **Embrace** them. To embrace something means to welcome it with open arms, hold, hug, accept completely. It means to squeeze (someone) tightly in your arms, usually with fondness.

There is something special about a warm embrace. It generates a feeling of security, love, and acceptance. It says, "I'm here for you", "I care about you", "I got you."

Where there are no embraces, there is no joy at all.

2. You **Cherish** them. In Gary Thomas' book, *Cherish,* he describes what it means to cherish someone. When we cherish someone, we naturally want to *protect* them – it could be physical protection, but also protection of an emotional or spiritual sort. We will *treat them with tenderness* because they matter so much to us.

We will look for ways to *nurture* them and occasionally go out of our way to *indulge* them. The thought of them will make us smile.

To cherish someone is to *hold them dear*. That means you think about them, and when you do, you feel great pleasure, you have great affection for them. You go out of your way to show they are important to you and you showcase them.

Men, your wives do not want you to just "love" them in the sense of being committed to them; they want you to cherish them. They want to hear "you are altogether beautiful, my darling, there is no flaw in you" (Song of Songs 4:7).

Women, you will discover that a cherished husband is the happiest of husbands. Cherishing your husband will help you dwell on his most excellent qualities, giving you greater satisfaction in marriage: "His mouth is sweetness itself; he is altogether lovely. This is my beloved; this is my friend…" (Song of Songs 5:16).

3. You **Learn how to Love them**. We love them, but do they *feel* loved? One of the difficulties in many of our marriages today (unlike in the Garden - before the Fall), is that we love (committed to the marriage); but do not always understand how to love (making our spouse feel loved).

One of the reasons our spouses do not understand how to make us *feel* loved, is because we are not always good at communicating what makes us feel loved in the first place. Often, we just "expect" our spouses to know how to create that "loving feeling" in our marriage relationship.

Gary Chapman, Ph.D., and author of *"The 5 Love Languages"* series, provides a quick guide to the five love languages in his book he wrote for Blended Families in partnership with Ron Deal, licensed marriage and family therapist and author of *The Smart Stepfamily*.

The book is titled, *"Building Love Together in Blended Families."* In this book Chapman explains that in *"The 5 Love Languages"* he uses the metaphor of literal languages to help readers understand that the way individuals perceive emotional love are so distinct from one another that they essentially comprise five different "languages" or channels of communication.

Each of us has at least one language that communicates emotional love to us more deeply than the others.

Chapman describes the 5 "languages", or "channels of communication" as follows:

Words of Affirmation - words that speak to the worth of the individual. The purpose is to affirm things you sincerely appreciate about the person. You must know however, a "words of affirmation person" can be emotionally devastated by insults and harsh words.

Quality Time - giving someone your full, undivided attention. The important thing is not "what" you are doing, but "why" you are doing it - to spend time together. You must know however, a "quality time person" can be hurt by halfhearted or distracted listening, or by repeatedly postponing promised time together.

Gifts or Receiving Gifts - giving someone something meaningful to them. It is the thoughtfulness and effort behind the gift that sends the "I love you" message. You must know however, a "gifts person" can be hurt by a forgotten anniversary or birthday, or left feeling empty in a relationship void of tangible tokens of love.

Acts of Service-doing things to help another person. Actions speak louder than words to those who have this love language. You must know that an "acts of service person" can be hurt by laziness, someone leaving a mess for them to clean up, or forgotten promises to help.

Physical Touch - connecting with someone physically. For some people, physical touch communicates most clearly "I love you." You must know however, for a "physical touch person", an angry shove or slap or other physical abuse can cause extreme emotional pain.

All of these are valid ways to express love to others. However, what makes one person feel loved does not necessarily make another person feel loved. The key is learning to speak the other person's love language.

Love them the way they need to be loved – the result? They will love you back!

In summary–the significance of the first response:

To finish up this learned Lesson #6–The First Response Says it All–*Your Appreciation Shows*, let us summarize what we have discussed:

1. Adam's first response when receiving his gift (the woman) was: *"At last! a suitable companion, a perfect partner!"* There was elation and excitement in Adam's response. He finally received the special gift he so desperately wanted. The first response says it all.

2. The principle of the first response is predicated on how one feels about the situation. Adam felt great about his gift, and so ecstatic, that it rubbed off on those involved in the exchange and they, also, walked away feeling good.

3. The first response can escalate an already bad moment. But a positive first response can bring calm, pleasantness, and the feeling of grateful appreciation. This would then elevate the intimacy in a relationship in an incredibly positive manner.

4. The first impression is predicated on what *you see* when you see something or someone. It is a lasting impression. How you first see someone will impact how you treat them.

5. What you call your spouse is what they will be. There is power in your tongue.

6. When you finally get that special gift (your loving companion) you always wanted; Embrace them. Appreciate them. Cherish them. Learn *how* to Love them.

7. If marriages today started like the "first marriage"–then love wouldn't fade, commitment wouldn't wane, and the "disrupter" of all things good would not win. Then divorce would no longer be an issue because **in the beginning it was not so!**

CHAPTER 9

Lesson 7: Special Instructions for Proper Handling – *Your Path to Oneness (Genesis 2:24, 25)*

"That is why a man leaves his father and mother and unites with his wife, and they become one family. The man and his wife were both naked, but they were not ashamed." (New English Translation)

Through the journey of the previous six lessons, we have traveled from the beginning of Adam to the naming of creatures, to the joy and excitement that resulted when Adam saw the "new" creature whom he called "woman."

These first six lessons centered around the man and woman as individuals, and then their joining together, modeling the "first" marriage ceremony. In that ceremony there were two people (Adam and Eve) who were created to complete each other, share intimacy, work side by side in child rearing, and reflect God's love to each other.

This "mystery" of marriage and marital oneness (see Ephesians 5:31-32) was created by God for humankind. Marriage was created with purpose.

In this final learned lesson, we will see how God establishes a path for the man and woman to now take together in their marriage relationship. These instructions, if followed, will provide a lifetime of happiness for them together as one "couple."

Couples who have decided to marry must realize that although they are still individuals, they are also now one "couple", and are responsible **to** and responsible **for** each other.

It is no longer just about you; it is now about the marriage relationship. That is why you "leave" and "cleave." You become one couple/team/unit!

The apostle Paul refers to Genesis when he says, "A man shall leave his father and mother and hold fast to his wife, and the two shall become one flesh" (Ephesians 5:31). Husband and wife are to live as one, united in love for God and for one another, modeling the love Christ has for His bride, the Church.

Tony Evans, in his Bible Commentary, explains this as follows: In marriage, a man and woman come together to make a new reality that God calls "one flesh." Thus, human relationships outside of the marriage bond are to be considered secondary - including the couple's relationships with their parents.

Unfortunately, too many couples never get around to becoming one flesh in this sense. They are stuck together by cheap glue rather than divine cement.

Numerous husbands and wives spend too much time protecting their own turf: my career versus your career, my money versus your money, my dreams versus your dreams. Yet, the purpose of marriage is to advance God's kingdom rule on earth for his glory.

This does not mean losing individuality. Rather, it means working together with your spouse for a joint goal. Husbands and wives need a bigger agenda that unites them: God's agenda. However, following it takes time, energy, humility, and sacrifice".

This Genesis scripture (2:24) outlines three key instructions for every successful marriage: Leaving Father and Mother; being United to Your Wife; Two becoming One Flesh. This is our path to "oneness."

Leaving Father and Mother:

The Hebrew verb translated "leave" normally means "to abandon, to forsake, to leave behind," when used with human subject and object (see Josh 22:3; 1 Sam 30:13; Prov 2:17; Isa 54:6; Jer. 49:11). Within the context of the ancient Israelite extended family structure however, this cannot refer to emotional or geographical separation.

It is hyperbole used to emphasize the change in perspective that typically overtakes a young man when his thoughts turn to love and marriage.

God has a reason for telling couples that are getting married to leave their father and mother. The significance is that our new marriage relationship must be stronger than the relationship with our extended family and friends.

The relationship with our spouse must be more important than, and must supersede, all other relationships in our lives, except our relationship with God.

Two people cannot become one if other people, such as parents, extended family members, friends, or former spouses, are allowed by one or both spouses to be involved in the decisions in their marriage.

Each spouses' relationship with their parents and others must change. The Bible tells us that parents and extended family are to be loved, honored, and respected. Parental advice can be of great value when asked for, but the married couple is no longer obligated to the parents.

Being United to Your Wife (Cleaving)

God instructs a man entering a marriage covenant to unite to his wife. Webster's definition of the word *unite* is "to couple; to cause to adhere; to attach; to incorporate in one; to ally; to join in interest and affection.

In Genesis 2:24 The verb "united to" is traditionally translated "cleaves [to]"; it has the basic idea of "stick with/to". *It describes the inseparable relationship between the man and the woman in marriage as God intended it.*

In fact, the closer we draw to God as individuals in this covenant, the closer we come to our mates; and then the closer we become in marriage, the more intimate we become with God.

Healthy, growing marriages seek to build on this foundation. Couples who place God at the center of their relationship, whether first, second, or third, put Him in charge of their wills, their choices, their money, their vocation, and their parenting.

Such couples, while never achieving marital perfection (that is not the goal), will undoubtedly experience some of God's richest blessings.

This inseparable relationship uniting these two individuals involves romantic affections, committed love, trust, a sense of companionship, a satisfying sexual relationship, healthy communication and conflict resolution skills, and a host of other qualities.

Just as Jesus gave His all for us because of His love and compassion for us, we are to develop the same "give it all" relationship with our spouse through the unity of our new relationship, and our commitment to join together in love and enduring affection.

Becoming One Flesh (Couple/Family)

Genesis 2:24 says, "….and they become one flesh." The Hebrew word refers to more than just a sexual union. The man and woman bring into being a new family unit. The phrase "one flesh" occurs only here and must be interpreted in light verse 23. There the man declares that the woman is bone of his bone and flesh of his flesh. To be one's "bone and flesh" is to be related by blood to someone.

The expression "one flesh" seems to indicate that they become, as it were, "kin," at least legally (a new family unit is created) or metaphorically. In this first marriage in human history, the woman was literally formed from the man's bone and flesh. God's creation from Adam's rib brought forth a suitable helper who was equal, opposite to, and together they became one flesh (one couple; one family).

The first marriage sets the pattern for how later marriages are understood and explains why marriage supersedes the parent-child relationship. (See New Testament use of this passage in Matt 19:5-6; Mark 10:8; 1 Cor 6:16; and Eph 5:31).

A Side Note:

There is a deeper correlation between the man and woman "becoming one." A broader purpose and more profound model of what "becoming one" in the marriage covenant suggests, and what is to be replicated in our marriage relationships.

God created both man and woman in the image of God. Jesus is equal to the Father but chose to submit to the Father and become our Savior. The Holy Spirit is equal to the Father and to Jesus, yet the Holy Spirit points us to Jesus and is our Helper – with us and in us (John 14:16).

The Three-in-One Godhead (the Trinity) exhibit no rivalry, competition, or inferiority, but are co-equal and fully God, working together to accomplish God's will and plan.

Marriage between a man and a woman is to model that kind of love, submissiveness, and unity.

What is a "Oneness" Relationship

Defined: The quality, state, or fact of being **one**; singleness of heart and mind; harmony; unity. Achieving oneness may seem far-fetched or impossible, but paraphrasing Genesis 2:24, it says that if spouses will leave other people out of their relationship, unite with each other, then the two will become one. In other words, doing the first two (leaving others and uniting) brings forth oneness.

Becoming "one", in a marriage relationship, is a process. It does not happen easily, and it does not happen overnight. The "pressure test" of time helps forge closer relationships if we allow the process to work for our good (see Romans 8:28).

In the book, *Preparing for Marriage,* it is stated: *"A 'oneness marriage' is the opposite of the world's 50/50 plan. It is a 100/100 plan in which both the husband and wife commit themselves totally to each other, set aside their own selfishness, and experience true intimacy. In the 100/100 plan, there is no talk about 'meeting each other halfway.' You are both willing to do anything it takes to make the marriage work."*

Jesus' prayer in John 17-*"That they may be one",* was a prayer Jesus prayed to His Father hours before the time of His death. His desire for "oneness" is for marriages, families, and for the universal church body, and should be our goal in all our key relationships.

The path to oneness as stated in Genesis 2:24, which speaks of a man leaving his parents to be united to, (or "be joined to") his wife, is a scripture read during many wedding ceremonies for good reason.

However, did those vows make the two of you "one" that day? Not likely. Rather, the vows you made on your wedding day are your commitment and promise to your spouse and to God to work to become one, and to remain faithful, true, and passionate toward each other.

The husband and wife are to become one in body, mind, and in spirit. We all understand the simplicity of becoming one in body, but many marriages and families struggle because they never become one in mind and/or spirit.

In fact, the most unhappy marriages are those in which the husband and wife are not one in mind or spirit. They have different interests, different goals, different beliefs, different ideas, and different agendas. They do not agree on anything of significance.

They do not enjoy doing the same things or, for that matter, enjoy being with each other. Nor do they support each other's dreams in life.

Please realize that spouses must become one. This must be the priority in any new marriage. Becoming one means being in one mind (harmony) and one purpose (direction) and having and setting common goals (vision).

A man and his new bride must do as the Bible says in Genesis 2:24 and leave father and mother (emotionally, financially, and psychologically), and all other external people, making it a priority to be united together intentionally developing a loving supportive partnership whereby the two grow together in oneness and unity.

As couples become "one" inseparable emotional union, experiencing "oneness" and closeness in the marriage relationship, the more intimate the relationship will become with one another, and will become with God. Afterall, He created it that way in the beginning!

Naked but Not Ashamed

In Genesis 2:25 it says, *"the man and his wife were both naked, but they were not ashamed."*

The idea of nakedness is introduced here at the end of the chapter. In the Bible nakedness conveys different things. In this context it signifies either innocence or integrity. There is no fear of exploitation, no sense of vulnerability. They were not created to know to be ashamed of their nakedness or to hide their true selves.

The love story in Eden began with Adam and Eve enjoying bone-of-my-bones, flesh-of-my-flesh intimacy. But the same two people who were naked and unashamed are, only a few verses later, trying to cover up their shame.

If you think of "naked" in the sense of open, honest, true, genuine, free, and trusting, you get a clearer picture of the beauty of this first marriage relationship. This first couple being naked "but they were not ashamed", is essential to understanding the intimate relationship God designed marriage to be. This goes far deeper than the presence or absence of clothing.

Yet, if we do make wearing "clothing" analogous to "covering or hiding our true selves", we begin to understand the significance of the first couple being "naked" and not "ashamed."

Think of being "ashamed" from the perspective of emotions. When people are ashamed, they hide themselves, or cover-up. If you are not ashamed (emotionally) you are innocent, open, honest, transparent; and vulnerable. This is what an emotionally healthy person enjoys, and on which an intimate marriage relationship is based.

Developing this type of emotional transparency and intimacy is the essence of "becoming one." It is a critical part of our path to oneness.

Here is an example of how "not being ashamed" impacts the marriage relationship.

(Carol) When Terry and I first got married he would come to bed fully clothed in his heavy two-piece thick pajamas. It was how he was used to sleeping and says it was a good way to cover his shapely body type (he continues to say, hey, round is a shape!). Me, on the other hand, I jump into the bed free of any garments at all (if you know what I mean), just as God intended, "naked and not ashamed." I have this "free spirit" of a personality who has no shame with my body, naked or otherwise! One evening I said to Terry, "man what's with the two-piece checkered thick pajamas?" "You are making me hot, and it's not in a good way, with those thick PJ's!"

That statement was so significant for our marriage. Because I then understood that us growing together into oneness had nothing to do with my round body shape or the looks of my body. There was no need to "hide" my body or feel ashamed. I can just be free to be me!

I began to realize that her love for me was a deep love that comes from her heart. Her acceptance of me as her husband was not based on the shape of my body, or the clothing I did or did not wear when coming to bed. It simply was *the connecting of our hearts*.

Carol's acceptance of me allowed me to understand the true meaning of being naked and not ashamed. It had nothing to do with the actual clothing of the body but the sheer genuineness of love that our father has for us as his children and we can have for, and with, each other.

What a joy to know that the love my wife has for me is not super-ficial. I can continue to get into our marital bed and feel the comfort of our bodies lovingly coming together freely as God intended. It is analogous to the emotionally unashamed *inti-macy* our marriage relationship enjoys.

What is intimacy?

Intimacy is closeness between people in personal relationships.

It is what builds over time as you connect with someone, grow to care about each other, and feel more and more comfortable during your time together.

It can include physical or emotional closeness, or even a mix of the two.

Intimacy is not synonymous with sex. You have probably heard of intimacy in the context of sex and romance. For example, people sometimes use the term "being intimate" to mean sexual activity. But intimacy is not another word for sex.

Sex with a partner *can* build intimacy, but it is far from the only indicator of intimacy. It is possible to have sex without intimacy as well as intimacy without sex.

How to nurture intimacy in any relationship

It is normal for relationships to feel stagnant over time as life gets in the way and you settle into a routine that is not as adventurous as when you first met.

Here are some ideas for sparking or reigniting intimacy in any relationship.

Make it a point to show your appreciation

Take time to tell the other person what you appreciate about them. Show your gratitude, which can take the form of gifts, favors, or a simple "thank you."

Make an effort to learn about each other

Once you have known someone for a long time, it can feel like the "mystery" is gone.

But people and relationships grow and change over time. There is always more to learn.

Swap stories, ask questions, and play games like "20 Questions" to keep gathering new information.

The key to this is listening so you can build a real understanding of what the other person cares about and why.

Set aside time for each other

If you are not paying attention, it is easy for time to fly by without sharing quality time.

So, make it a priority!

Plan a weekly date night, a monthly board game night, or a nightly moment to check in one-on-one before bedtime, away from the kids or other responsibilities.

Unplug and focus on each other

Spending time together without electronics can give you a chance to give each other some undivided attention.

Show physical affection (even without sex)

If you have a sexual relationship, then mixing things up with new toys, outfits, and fantasies can keep things from getting dull.

But you can also build intimacy by making it a point to show physical affection without sex.

With warm gestures and cuddles, you can remember that joining your bodies together is about more than just "getting off."

Tackle a project together

Restore a piece of furniture, learn a new skill like baking, or teach your old dog some new tricks.

Whatever the project, working toward a goal with a loved one can cultivate bonding time, make invaluable memories, and give you something new to look forward to together.

Talk about what intimacy means to you

Building intimacy does not have to be a guessing game.

An easy way to figure out how to build intimacy is to just talk about it!

Tell your loved one how you would like to spend time together and what activities help you feel closer. Listen when they tell you the same.

Building intimacy is one of the most rewarding ways to enrich your life. Give yourself permission to seek out the meaningful connections you deserve.

In summary-the significance of oneness:

To finish up this learned Lesson #7-Special Instructions for Proper Handling-*Your Path to Oneness*, let us summarize what we have discussed:

1. God has established a path for man and woman to take together to build a oneness relationship. These instructions, if followed, will provide them a lifetime of happiness together, as one "couple."

2. Genesis 2:24 outlines three key instructions for every successful marriage: Leaving Father and Mother; being United to Your Wife; Two becoming One Flesh.

3. Couples getting married are to leave their father and mother. The new marriage relationship must be stronger than the relationship with extended family and friends.

4. God instructs a man entering a marriage covenant to unite to his wife. It describes the *inseparable* relationship between the man and the woman in marriage as God intended it.

5. Spouses must become one. This must be the priority in any new marriage. Becoming one means being in one mind, one purpose, and having and setting common goals.

6. The first couple was naked "but they were not ashamed." Not ashamed means, you are innocent, open, honest, transparent; and vulnerable. This is what an emotionally healthy person enjoys, *and on which an intimate marriage relationship is based.*

7. Intimacy is closeness between people in personal relationships. It is what builds over time as you connect with someone, grow to care about each other, and feel more and more comfortable during your time together.

CHAPTER 10

Tips and Tools

10A. What Submission Really Means (Carol)

The dictionary defines submission as "the action or fact of accepting or yielding to a superior force, or will, or authority of another person. The legalistic application of the concept of submission leads to bullying, heartache, and divorce. That is not God's vision for marriage, so that belief cannot be the correct interpretation of what it means to submit.

In layman's terms submitting means: putting others before yourself; it means not always doing what you want; it means putting God's desires above your desires.

In her book, *Every Reason to Leave, author Vickie Rose stated, "Wives, submission means understanding your power and using it in a way that builds your husband's leadership. After 37 years of marriage, I can tell you that I have discovered that there is joy and peace in submission. When I have submitted to my husband's leadership, God has poured out so much blessing, and He has been glorified."

The issue with submission comes when there is the issue of 'ego'. Submission involves letting go of our egos and rights. When we lay our egos and rights at the Lord's feet, we will be submitting automatically without considering it a big deal. I would like to rephrase this verse saying that "let not your egos and rights prevent you from doing what the Lord wants you to do."

God wants wives to please their husbands through their submission and husbands through their loving. Loving is not possible without submission or submission without loving.

Five important factors men need to understand about submission

1. Submission in marriage always begins with MUTUAL submission to Christ.

This passage about how husbands and wives should act and interact in marriage begins with a call to mutual submission in Christ (Ephesians 5:21) *"submit to one another out of reverence for Christ."* God is the head of the marriage and ultimate leader and authority. If we are not submitting to His word and His will, we will never be able to live, lead or love the way God intended.

2. God is offended when his daughters are mistreated or bullied.

Men, did you know that one of the few behaviors the Bible lists as something that will hinder your prayers is being harsh with your wife? (1 Peter 3:7) *"husbands, in the same way be considerate as you live with your wives, and treat them with respect as the weaker partner and as heirs with you of the gracious gift of life, so that nothing will hinder your prayers."*

The tone of your words will shape the tone of your marriage. God is giving husbands a clear mandate to treat your wives with tenderness, respect, support, and encouragement.

3. **It is never a husband's job to "make" his wife submit.**

Scripture never instructs the husband to enforce anything over his wife. In fact, the Bible warns of gentiles (unbelievers) who lord authority over others. In Christ, leadership is about serving. Yes, husbands are given a unique mandate to lead and a responsibility to be accountable for the family, and while a Godly wife should respect her husband and submit to him as the Bible instructs, how she ultimately chooses to (or not to) submit is something only God can enforce, reward, or punish. Nowhere in Scripture is a husband told to enforce a behavior with his wife. That would create a parent-child dynamic instead of the equal partnership God intends for marriage.

4. **Husbands are called to submit MORE than wives.**

Your mission as husbands is to "…love your wife as Christ loved the church." He gave his very life for men. He pursued you when you denied him, he loved you when you were unlovable, he gave his best when you could not repay, and he died to his own desires and wants to give life and then told you to love your wives with that same kind of love. That is humbling; and doing the same requires a lot of submission on your part.

5. **Our marriage mission is not submission but it's love.**

In practical terms, Christ-like love should compel husbands to daily lay down their own demands to willingly pursue the preferences of your wives. Let us be free to be who God shaped and gifted us to be. Love your wives enough to study their likes, dislikes, fears and even their shame. As Jesus washed his disciples' feet, get some good lotion, and sometimes massage your wife's feet. Delight in seeing her smile knowing she has a husband who adores her.

Men if you do these things, you both will be more content in your marriage and your wife will feel cherished, loved, and adored. When there comes a crossroad in your marriage or when you and your wife are not in complete agreement about which road to take, she will find it so much easier to be submissive to your Godly leadership. Because she knows without a doubt, she has a husband who is following the Lord, and who would gladly give his life for her.

Every Reason to Leave, Vicki Rose, Copyright 2014, Moody Publishers, 820 N. Lasalle Boulevard, Chicago, IL.

10B. How Love Behaves

1 Corinthians 13:4-8

[4] Love is **patient** - able to endure displeasure for a long time. Be wronged and not retaliate

Love is **kind** - having a merciful attitude toward someone who has wronged us

It does not **envy** - always wanting what you don't have; unwilling to share what you do have

It does not **boast** - does not strut, parade itself, brag, show off; always anxious to impress

It is not **proud** - arrogant, conceited, swelled head. Does not have an inflated view of self

[5] It does not **dishonor others** - not rude or disrespectful to others

It is not **self-seeking** - not selfish, not its "me-first" and "me always"

It is not **easily angered**-does not fly off the handle; is not easily provoked

It keeps **no record of wrongs** - does not keep score of the sins of others

[6] Love does **not delight in evil** - does not rejoice in injustice or wrongdoing, by you or others

but **rejoices with the truth** - that which is in accord with reality and therefore accurate and trustworthy

[7] It always **protects** - do you protect your spouse from harm, or do you do the harming?

always **trusts**-do you more readily believe and trust, or generally regard people with suspicion?

always **hopes**-do you expect negative outcomes from people, or believe in God's ability to change them?

always **endures**-do you choose to act in loving ways, even when you do not feel you can keep loving?

[8] Love **never fails**-never ends! Never falls short! Love keeps going to the end!

1 Corinthians 13 (Amplified Bible)

The Excellence of Love

[1] If I speak with the tongues of men and of angels but have not love [for others growing out of God's love for me], then I have become only a noisy gong or a clanging cymbal [just an annoying distraction]. [2] And if I have *the gift of* prophecy [and speak a new message from God to the people], and understand all mysteries, and [possess] all knowledge; and if I have all [sufficient] faith so that I can remove mountains, but do not have love [reaching out to others], I am nothing. [3] If I give all my possessions to feed *the poor*, and if I surrender my body to be burned, but do not have love, it does me no good at all.

[4] Love endures with patience *and* serenity, love is kind *and* thoughtful, and is not jealous *or* envious; love does not brag

and is not proud *or* arrogant. **5** It is not rude; it is not self-seeking; it is not provoked [nor overly sensitive and easily angered]; it does not take into account a wrong *endured*. **6** It does not rejoice at injustice but rejoices with the truth [when right and truth prevail]. **7** Love bears all things [regardless of what comes], believes all things [looking for the best in each one], hopes all things [remaining steadfast during difficult times], endures all things [without weakening].

8 Love never fails [it never fades nor ends]. But as for prophecies, they will pass away; as for tongues, they will cease; as for the gift of special knowledge, it will pass away. **9** For we know in part, and we prophesy in part [for our knowledge is fragmentary and incomplete]. **10** But when that which is complete *and* perfect comes, that which is incomplete *and* partial will pass away. **11** When I was a child, I talked like a child, I thought like a child, I reasoned like a child; when I became a man, I did away with childish things. **12** For now [in this time of imperfection] we see in a mirror dimly [a blurred reflection, a riddle, an enigma], but then [when the time of perfection comes, we will see reality] face to face. Now I know in part [just in fragments], but then I will know fully, just as I have been fully known [by God]. **13** And now there remain: faith [abiding trust in God and His promises], hope [confident expectation of eternal salvation], love [unselfish love for others growing out of God's love for me], these three [the choicest graces]; but the greatest of these is love.

Footnote:

1 Corinthians 13:1-a profound thoughtfulness and unselfish concern for other believers regardless of their circumstances or station in life. Terry Moss – April 2021

10C. Ten Ways to Reflect God's Humility

What a wonderful loving and humble God we serve. Thankfully, the Bible includes much guidance on how to practice His humility on earth.

1. Humbly acknowledge God in everything

For the sake of our own souls, we need to regularly bow our hearts to our magnificent, awe-inspiring, and humble God. There are no human words that can describe who He is and how He has blessed us.

Psalm 8:3-4 ESV When I look at your heavens, the work of your fingers, the moon, and the stars, which you have set in place, what is man that you are mindful of him, and the son of man that you care for him?

Let us make it a point to always ask God for His will humbly for all our plans and decisions. When we presume, we know what is right, we fall into idolatry because it sets us above God's will.

Proverbs 3:7 ESV Do not be wise in your own eyes; Fear the LORD and turn away from evil.

2. Confess and repent of pride

Pride will not allow God to sit on the throne in our hearts to rule over and redeem our past, present, and future. This will eventually destroy us. Let us humbly repent for our pride and all the times we have tried to control our own lives in the false belief that we have the power to.

Romans 12:3 NLT … Do not think you are better than you really are. Be honest in your evaluation of yourselves, measuring your-selves by the faith God has given us.

3. Thank God every day

It is God's will that we thank Him in any circumstance because He knows this helps us keep our hearts in check. As we humble ourselves, we will be surprised by how long our lists can be if we truly are thankful.

1 Thessalonians 5:18 ESV give thanks in all circumstances; for this is the will of God in Christ Jesus for you.

Let us not hesitate to deflect any praise we receive and make it a point to thank our Father in heaven instead. He is the true Source of all our talents and gifts.

4. Stop grumbling

Any form of grumbling, whining, or protesting stems from a spirit of self-entitlement and self-righteousness. When we humble our hearts and submit to God instead, we will be posi-tive shining lights in our world.

Philippians 2:14-15 ESV Do all things without grumbling or questioning, that you may be blameless and innocent, children of God without blemish in the midst of a crooked and twisted generation, among whom you shine as lights in the world.

5. Stop passing judgment

We all have the tendency to conclude certain things about other people, not realizing that we are, passing judgment on them. It is even worse if we conclude that "they will never change" or "they are beyond hope". Not only do we judge them, but we also curse them. Such judgmental pride assumes we are all-knowing and entitled to condemn others. It also implies that God cannot work a miracle in their lives. This slander and offends our all-powerful and merciful Father in heaven. This is something we need to actively avoid.

Matthew 7:1 ESV Judge not, that you be not judged. For with the judgment you pronounce you will be judged, and with the measure you use it will be measured to you.

6. Stop boasting

Pride tells us we deserve recognition for our achievements, sacrifices and giving. In some sense, we wish to be worshipped; neglecting that God alone deserves all worship. God promises to reward those who humbly wait on His personal praises, and not crave the recognition and praises of other people. Let us serve, love, and sacrifice joyfully, without seeking the approval of people.

2 Corinthians 10:17-18 ESV Let the one who boasts, boast in the Lord. For it is not the one who commends himself who is approved, but the one whom the Lord commends.

7. Stop seeking attention

Some people enjoy drawing attention to themselves by being pushy, boastful, crude, or antagonistic. All this behavior is driven by the innate belief that other people should listen to or follow them. Humility, on the other hand, will gently consider others first.

Philippians 2:4 ESV Let each of you look not only to his own interests, but also to the interests of others.

Ephesians 4:2 ESV with all humility and gentleness, with patience, bearing with one another in love…

8. Admit mistakes and weaknesses readily

The fear of admitting our faults and vulnerabilities is driven by a desire to protect our personal image. We idolize our reputations at the expense of God's. Like the apostle Paul, we should not be afraid of exposing our personal weaknesses, so that people will see Jesus' Holy Spirit working in us. This takes true strength as well as true humility.

2 Corinthians 12:9 ESV but he said to me, "My grace is sufficient for you, for my power is made perfect in weakness." Therefore, I will boast even more gladly of my weaknesses, so that the power of Christ may rest upon me.

9. Consider others as more important

The thought of considering others first is most unnatural to human beings. Even as children, we loathe to share our candy and toys. True humility is demonstrated when we do just the opposite. It shows our hearts to be free of fears and selfish intentions. We can love those whom God loves, regardless of how they behave towards us. Jesus set the perfect example by humbly dying on the cross for all of us.

Philippians 2:3 ESV Do nothing from selfish ambition or conceit, but in humility count others more significant than yourselves.

10. Forgive and bless others

The choice to forgive and bless those who offend us is a true test of our humility and submission to God. The Bible tells us to pray for and bless others, especially those whom we see as our enemies. It does not tell us to *try* to bless our abusers, it simply tells us to just do it.

Ephesians 4:32 ESV Be kind to one another, tenderhearted, forgiving one another, as God in Christ forgave you.

Luke 6:27-28 ESV But I say to you who hear, Love your enemies, do good to those who hate you, bless those who curse you, pray for those who abuse you.

Unforgiveness is a form of pride that implies we are better than other people and deserve only worship and adoration. This pride keeps us from being good representatives of a humble God who sent His Son to die for us. In contrast, we are to actively bless those we are inclined to hate, resent, or find intolerable, so that they get to experience the wonderful grace of the humble perfect God we serve.

BY JENNIFER SUM • PUBLISHED 2015-05-19

https://teachinghumblehearts.com/en/category/Christianity/practice/humility/

Conclusion

Well, what a journey! What great revelation coming from the Garden! This was learned truth that can transform our lives and our relationships.

God's intent for marriage is so beautifully detailed in the Garden of Eden. But of course, what is revealed in the Garden is going to be beautiful, that is what a garden is, beautiful!

How refreshing to see and give meaning to the intents of the Designer's heart as each learned lesson unfolded. There was meaning and intentionality in each lesson. God indeed had a purpose for his human creation to connect deeply, love unselfishly, and enjoy the intimacy of marriage in relationship forever.

Hopefully, this work has provided you dear readers the model for enjoying fulfilling marriages as intended from the beginning.

No longer will you have to wonder how to do marriage right. Now, regardless of the inadequate models you have seen in the past, or the inadequate marriage you have experienced yourself until now, this book can be your path to a oneness marriage like you have never experienced before.

Prayerfully accept the truths revealed in this book. Continue to seek wisdom from these inspired words daily as you learn new ways to live out these principles and enjoy your marriage relationship more fully and successfully.

The task may seem daunting. Unlearning old habits and then relearning new ones is challenging work. But be assured, the labor of love is worth every effort. This is your time to be stretched, be challenged, and to be transformed.

The new you with a new perspective, connected to your spouse with the same purpose and perspective, will produce a marriage relationship like the "first couple" experienced in the Garden.

Now is your time to *be the model* of a healthy, fulfilling marriage relationship. Your children and your children's children need to see what this looks like. We do not want this generation to sit on the counselor's couch in the future, stating what many have stated in our time, "I just have not seen any models of healthy, fulfilling marriages the way God intended."

Let your marriage relationship BE THE MODEL!

Afterword:
You Can Do This!

If *someone* can do a thing, then *anyone* can do it. That is a great statement! The meaning is profound. If someone can do a thing, that is proof that the thing *can* be done.

Therefore, as concerning marriage, if someone has implemented the truths learned in the Garden, then that is proof that it is possible to do, and that these truths must work.

There are countless marriages that do work. Some work by chance, some work by choice. We (the authors) have experienced the joy of relationship that comes from doing marriage the way God intended in the Garden. It works!

This is your challenge. Begin implementing the truths learned in this book, that were detailed from the Garden. But know this, to do them you must understand what has been revealed during the journey through this book. Here are a few gems:

1. God created man and then fashioned the woman – on purpose, for His purpose. They were pure, innocent, loving, and connected – from the beginning.

The truth revealed: We must have a transformed heart and renewed mind to get back to the "pure innocence" of the first couple. We have developed hardened hearts and calloused minds that must be softened and changed. God can "recreate" as well as "create." Let Him do it in you. Just ask Him. Go ahead, you can do it!

2. Man and Woman embraced their purpose to fulfill their promise. The man appreciated and cherished the woman – the woman understood her role and submitted (naturally) to the leadership of her husband.

The truth revealed: God created the man and woman with the intuitive nature to love and respect one another. They had His nature instilled in them! With a newly created heart and mind, you now have the same ability, instilled in you, to love and cherish your wife (husband); and the ability to come alongside to help, and respectfully submit to the leadership of your husband (wife).

3. It is not good for man (mankind) to be *alone*. We were created to be in relationship. That is as true today as it was in the beginning.

The truth revealed: Any man or woman can remain single (alone) and be fine. As a matter of fact, many people prefer to be *left alone* (do not bother me). But to enjoy the fullness that life has to offer, it must be done in relationship. Being alone (absence of relationship) is a lonely existence. Some believe it is the fact that they are *not* alone which is causing all their problems. They blame the spouse for their unhappiness. Full disclosure – you really are not as "in touch" with yourself or the world around you without relationship. A "loner" who refuses any type of human interaction will only have themselves by which to measure growth and maturity. How many of us are skilled at that?

The mirror of our true selves is the reflection from those in close relationship with us.

Our Prayer for You and Your Marriage

Our Father, we thank you for what you have revealed to us and in us, as your words came alive throughout this journey. We pray Father that your work continues in every heart to be the best of who you have designed us to be.
Bless each marriage so that they will reflect your purpose.
Let the wisdom of your word illuminate each heart and every mind, so that as these couples grow, we pray they grow in relationships that honor you.
Bring Love, Life, Laughter and Hope to each one.

Help us to follow your perfect plan, in perfect obedience to you. May we remain humble enough to ask for forgiveness and wise enough to grant It. Help us daily to remember your Words. They are light and they are Life.
Keep us from all harm when the "disrupter" tries to exert harm upon us. Let us forever give glory to your name because we represent you.
Bless our marriages and transform our hearts so both become accurate reflections of the very nature of you. In your Son's name we pray. Amen!

The Lord bless you and keep you; the Lord make his face shine upon you and be gracious to you; the Lord turn his face toward you and give you peace. (Numbers 6:24-26)

Many Blessings!
Terry & Carol

About the Authors

On the surface, it looks like Terry and Carol are total opposites. For that reason, who would have ever expected them to marry each other!

Carol is a strong, independent woman, with a great sense of humor and a servant's heart. She is also what is playfully called, "hip-hop and happening." She is the life of the party, and a fun-loving free spirit. Terry is like that loveable "nerdy guy"; intelligent, organized, focused, and loves to read. He has that "conservative church-boy Terry" persona.

Both have experienced the pain of divorce—Terry after 26 years; Carol after four years ending with domestic violence. Both also have experienced the redeeming work of God's grace. And what they both have learned about themselves and about marriage and relationships has not just come from formal training, but from their real-life experiences. They share these experiences with countless others continually.

How did this union come to be? It started with what has been called the most significant request of a lifetime; when Terry simply prayed, "Father, present to me, the woman you have prepared, to be my suitable helper." After a few short weeks, under the providence and direction from the Father above, there was a phone call and then dinner with Carol, a brief dating period, and five months later they were joined together; and their beautiful marriage relationship began, barefoot, on the beach, in the Bahamas!

Now Terry and Carol have been married to each other for nearly fifteen years. They are highly active in ministry to couples, centered around building healthy marriages through counseling, coaching, mentoring, teaching, and training. Within the last seven years they have added a focus around ministry to Blended Families (or Stepfamilies).

Terry and Carol are Certified Marriage Mentors in connection with the American Association of Christian Counselors, and Certified SYMBIS Facilitators through Drs. Les and Leslie Parrott Ministries. They also help build healthy marriage relationships through *One Flesh Ministries*, a marriage relationship building ministry in which they are Founders and Executive Officers.

One Flesh Ministries provides one-on-one marriage counseling (virtual and in-person), marriage coaching and mentoring, marriage intensives, as well as the facilitating of marriage conferences, retreats, workshops, and seminars. Terry and Carol are also Group Coordinators for FamilyLife, a CRU Ministry organization that has provided resources, help, and hope for marriages, and families for over 45 years.

These two have been described by couples who know them as: dedicated, sincere, authentic, trustworthy, experienced, wise, people of integrity, energetic, and fun-loving. They love life, love people, and love God who continues to be gracious and loving to them.

In addition to his 50+ years of ministry experience and Biblical teaching, Terry retired from Corporate America in 2018, after 46 years. When he retired, Terry was the Second Vice President of Commercial Underwriting for a large widely recognized Insurance Company. He has a B.A. Degree in Business Management and an extensive minor in Psychology.

Carol retired from the Federal Government in 2016. She retired as a Title 16 Technical Expert for the Social Security Administration after 31 years of service. Carol has led various church ministries including Hospitality, Ushers and Greeters, and Security Team ministries.

Carol also has her own Catering Company lovingly called, *"Carol's Kitchen."* Terry and Carol are members of Christ Fellowship Church in Palm Beach Gardens, Florida.

They enjoy traveling together and relaxing at home when given the opportunity. Terry also enjoys reading, watching sports, teaching, mentoring, and shepherding. Carol's gift of hospitality is expressed in her love for cooking, catering, event planning, and entertaining. They have been blessed with five children (one resides in heaven) and two grandchildren.

Carol's Expressions of Love

My joy and fulfillment working alongside my husband in the writing of this book is from a strong desire to have Terry's heart for God and Godly marriages memorialized and written on pages. Terry is such a great man; he demonstrates this in his lifestyle, his teachings, his coaching couples, his compassion for people, and leading of men. It is also proven in the way he loves me as his wife and the love he has for our children and our children's children.

These awesome qualities are currently being enjoyed by his family, friends and those God leads to him. My desire is for Terry to be able to leave his heart, his love, his obedience, and passion for Godly marriages, as written on the pages of this book, to be shared from generation to generation.

The character found in who Terry is today, needs to be left for us all long after he, one day, meets his heavenly Father. His life and current marriage are a true example of God's creation and intention for marriages. Terry is truly regarded like King Solomon, who God blessed with Wisdom and Knowledge. This book will leave a legacy of those blessings, which have been written on pages, to be shared with all God's people in this world and the world to come.

Bibliography

Throughout this book there are many Scripture references from the Holy Bible. Various versions were used to provide as much practical understanding and meaning as possible. No one version is being suggested as more accurate than another.

1. Richards, Lawrence. *New International Encyclopedia of Bible Words*, "Marriage." Grand Rapids: *Zondervan* Publishing House, 1985, 1991.

2. Johnson, John, Selfishness. January 15, 2015 https://www.psychologytoday.com/us/blog/cui-bono/201501/good-neutral-and-bad-selfishness, (Accessed 30 Oct 2020).

3. Dondas, Corina. "Traits of Selfishness." *Psychology Today*, September 6, 2019. ALLWOMENSTALK.com https://lifestyle.allwomenstalk.com/signs-of-a-selfish-person-that-you-should-pay-attention-to/, (Accessed 30 Oct 2020).

4. Fisher, Richard, "Why Is Marriage a "Mystery" in Ephesians 5?", *Revive Magazine,* November 1, 2017. https://lifeaction.org/why-is-marriage-a-mystery/, (Accessed 20 Nov 2020).

5. Warren, Rick. *The Purpose Driven Life*. Grand Rapids: Zondervan, 2002.

6. Robson, John. "Know, Grow and Flow Through Life." Higher Awareness. https://www.higherawareness.com/johnrobson. html (Accessed: 20 Nov 2020).

7. Soghomonian, Ida. "Boundaries–Why are They Important?" The Resilience Centre. https://www.theresiliencecentre. com.au/boundaries-why-are-they-important/ (Accessed 04 Dec 2020).

8. Selva, Joaquín. "How to Set Healthy Boundaries: 10 Examples + PDF Worksheets." Positive Psychology.com. https://positivepsychology.com/great-self-care-setting-healthy-boundaries/ (Accessed 10 May 2021).

9. Oliver, Jacqui. "Why Boundaries are Good." https://www. lifehack.org/854918/boundaries-in-marriage (Accessed 04 Dec 2020).

10. Jamieson, Fausset & Brown. "Commentary on Genesis 2." https://www.blueletterbible.org/Comm/jfb/Gen/Gen_002. cfm (Accessed 29 Jan 2021).

11. McLeod, Saul. "Maslow's Hierarchy of Needs." *Simply Psychology*, updated December 29, 2020. https://www. simplypsychology.org/maslow.html#gsc.tab=0 (Accessed 05 Feb 2021).

12. Goldsmith, Barton. "10 Ways to Get Your Needs Met." *Psychology Today*, February 16, 2016. https://www.psychologytoday.com/us/blog/emotional-fitness/201602/10-ways-get-your-needs-met (Accessed 05 Feb 2021).

13. Raypole, Crystal. "10 Emotional Needs." Healthline. https:// www.healthline.com/health/emotional-needs (Accessed 05 Feb 2021).

14. First Impression. "First Impressions." Psychology Today. https://www.psychologytoday.com/us/basics/first-impressions (Accessed 12 Feb 2021).

15. Thomas, Gary. *Cherish*. Grand Rapids: Zondervan, 2017.

16. Chapman, Gary, Ron L. Deal. *Building Love Together in Blended Families*. Chicago: Northfield Publishing, 2020.

17. Evans, Tony. *The Tony Evans Bible Commentary.* Nashville: Holman Bible Publishers, 2019.

18. Deal, Ron L. *The Smart Stepfamily*. Bloomington: Bethany House Publishers, 2014.

19. *Boehi, David, Brent Nelson, Jeff Schulte, and Lloyd Shadrach. Preparing for Marriage.* Ventura: Gospel Light, 1997.

20. Johnson, Maisha. "How to Understand and Build Intimacy in Every Relationship." Healthline. https://www.healthline.com/health/intimacy (Accessed 12 Mar 2021).

CPSIA information can be obtained
at www.ICGtesting.com
Printed in the USA
LVHW090050260621
691196LV00001B/2